VOTE.com

VOTE.COM

DICK MORRIS

RENAISSANCE BOOKS
Los Angeles

to Eileen McGann

Library of Congress Catalog Card Number: 99-067457
ISBN: 1-58063-105-3

10 9 8 7 6 5 4 3 2 1

Design by Susan Shankin

Published by Renaissance Books
Distributed by St. Martin's Press
Manufactured in the United States of America
First Edition

Acknowledgments

OPEN TO NEW IDEAS, intrigued by those who contradict the conventional wisdom, anxious to promote books that speak out, Renaissance Books is a publishing company to treasure.

Bill Hartley, the publisher, insists on innovation. Arthur Morey, who has become a friend as well as an editor (an unlikely combination), did a great job of helping me weave together several strands of this book into one narrative. Like the strands of DNA, he intertwined them to maximum effect. He combines a sharp pencil with an equally sharp wit, which makes his pencil the more palatable. Mike Dougherty, their marketing director, loves to challenge the establishment with new ideas. Ann Hartley did a magnificent job of helping to translate this book into English. She calls what she does "copy editing." And with Lisa Lenthall designing the book jacket, I can only hope that people will, indeed, judge this book by its cover.

Thank you all so very, very much.

Contents

THIS BOOK explains how, by means of the Internet, the Fifth Estate—a new political force—is about to transform American politics. The Fifth Estate is a sort of committee of the whole, made up of all citizens online. The author will probe how the rise of Internet democracy represents the triumph of people's politics over the power of intermediaries, particularly the power of the press and broadcast media, who make up the Fourth Estate. For the first time since the early nineteenth century, the United States is departing from the Madisonian model of representative government to return to Jefferson's radical concept of direct democracy.

The Internet will permit a candidate to target his message to distinct voting groups. The vast array of Web sites, each with its own singular area of content, will make it far easier for politicians to send relevant messages to each voter about his or her own particular interests. How the interactivity of the Internet will tell candidates—and their managers—what is working and what isn't.

How, as with talk-radio shows today, Internet campaigning will be interactive.

How e-mail campaigns will be crammed into the final hours before election day as last-minute appeals for votes volley back and forth.

How, a decade from now, politics could revolve around one-on-one virtual conversations between candidate and voter. The cybercandidate will be a composite of stored video images with preprogrammed responses.

Why voting over the Net will increasingly replace traditional polling. How this will let voters initiate ideas and assume an active role in the dialogue.

with one voice, ignoring national boundaries. In totalitarian countries like China, the Internet will pave the way for an expression of opinion that will challenge authority.

The power structure will not give way easily. Initially, members of the traditional media, the Fourth Estate, will ignore Internet democracy then will seek to discredit it. These struggles will be the battlefields of democracy in the next decade.

After Internet democracy has reallocated power, the pendulum will swing back to representative democracy, but only after the *vox populi* has been heard.

The evolution from the Fourth Estate to the Fifth Estate was only partially driven by the possibilities offered by the technology of the Internet. As much as the Internet attracted us, the journalism and politics of the Fourth Estate have come to repel us.

Ever since the fall of the traditional party bosses, the Fourth Estate has exerted control over elected officials. Its interpretations of political events and personalities has had an immense effect on elections.

perception of partisanship in the unimpeachment and increased public disdain for Congress.

How the modern presidency has become a Fifth Estate institution while Congress remains mired in the practices of the Fourth Estate. Why Congress is losing respect as voters realize that special interests control their representatives and dictate how they vote.

The wisdom of the few may be the light of mankind;
but the interest of the few is not the profit of mankind.

—JAMES HARRINGTON, 1656

INTRODUCTION

THERE HAS BEEN a quiet but radical revolution shaking the very foundation of our politics. While the television blares in the living rooms of America and the magazines and newspapers pile up beside the couch, Americans are quietly tapping away on their home computers—tuning in to the Internet. Bank.com, Travel.com, Shopping.com, RealEstate.com, and a hundred other businesses on tens of thousands of new Web sites are changing every aspect of American life. As tens of millions of people tune out the nightly network television news and stop dirtying their fingers with newsprint, they are using the Internet as their prime source of news and information about the outside world. News.com is increasingly opening the eyes of America to pluralistic input, different opinions, new information, and a wealth of news that even the most prolific of newspapers cannot match.

Through the expansion of the Internet, the proliferation of cable television news channels, and the inundation of information that cascades down upon us from new sources, our ears have grown larger, bringing us more input than ever before. But as our ears have grown, our mouths have remained the same. We have had a rapid growth in input without any corresponding change in our capacity to speak out. Our output is still confined to biannual excursions to the voting booth to render our decisions on our future. Just as the voting curtain confines us in a small space, so the choices available to us are increasingly inadequate to express the depth, passion, scope, and specificity of the opinions we have formed amid this deluge of information.

Now the interactivity that the technology of the Internet allows is about to send the information revolution into reverse. By permitting us to speak back to political figures, the Net will increase, exponentially, our capacity to participate in all levels of government. *Vote.com* is a metaphor for this new power that technology is about to place at the disposal of the average American. It will help our mouths, voices, throats, and lungs to grow as large as our ears and eyes have expanded in the information age.

Two hundred years ago, Thomas Jefferson had to shelve his vision of a direct democracy in which people made their own decisions at town meetings. The twin challenges of vast distances and limited communications made it necessary for us to select special people among us to go to places like Richmond, Albany, Harrisburg, Atlanta, and Washington, D.C., to make decisions for us.

Now we are about to reclaim the power Jefferson would have given us. Through the technology of the Internet, we have overcome the logistics that defeated Jefferson. Again we can move in the direction his vision would have led—toward direct democracy.

All across our society, the Internet is eliminating intermediaries. When we realized that stockbrokers were taking large commissions on our investments, we turned to the Internet to invest directly. We bypassed travel agents' commissions and purchased air tickets online. We are banking online rather than waiting on line at the bank. We are increasingly buying our clothing, food, pharmaceuticals, books, compact discs, and a long list of other products through the Internet without ever setting foot in a store. Now the Internet will eliminate the intermediaries in politics.

Our ability to use the Internet to express our views, not just to receive information, is in its infancy. As it matures, it will bring a new era to American politics. Almost nothing will be the same again. A plethora of Web sites are springing up giving Americans the ability to vote on the important issues that arise throughout the land. Already the Web sites for ABC, CBS, FOX, CNN, and MSNBC let people vote and express their views on some issues.

This book's namesake, Vote.com, is a new Web site that my wife, Eileen McGann, and I are founding that will not only encourage voting, but will also link your vote with e-mails to congressmen, senators, governors, and even the president. As soon as you vote, the officials who matter are automatically and immediately notified of your position and your opinion. How should we use the budget surplus? What is the best way to protect Social Security? Do we need to raise defense spending? Do we want national education standards? How about stricter gun controls? The answers will come cascading down on Congress as first hundreds of thousands and then millions and then tens of millions of people log on and express their opinions. Vote.com will also let people speak out on nonpolitical topics from who should win the Oscars to whether Prince Charles should marry Camilla.

The technology of the Internet enables massive political change. But it is the failure of the current players in politics and journalism that moves us to walk through the door that science has opened and take our government into our own hands. As we shall see later in this book, once the political bosses lost their power in the late 1960s and early 1970s, a nexus of journalists and their allies took over. The press, called the Fourth Estate by Edmund Burke at the end of the eighteenth century, told us what to think, how to behave, and how to respond to the events they reported.

But the Fourth Estate has blown it. It has alienated Americans who now long to cast aside the intermediaries—such as the journalists and broadcasters who manage the flow of information to us and the politicians who claim to express our resulting national consensus—and to get data and express their views directly over the Internet. This newly empowered majority is the Fifth Estate.

We have come to see the media as biased, self-involved, and isolated from the real world. In the recent failure to convict the president—the unimpeachment—only 16 percent of all Americans said that the media coverage was fair and free from pro- or anti-Clinton bias. To replace the media, we demand direct, primary sources of information, as diverse as possible. We want to make up our own minds. Predigested analyses of what's happening, by pundits who seek our proxy, are as unattractive as prefab meals. We insist on the right to sift through the raw material on our own. We Americans are increasingly thinking for ourselves.

On television, ABC, CBS, and NBC no longer rule. While in 1978, 90 percent of American households were tuned in to their programming, only 45 percent are now. As the audience for networks has declined, network influence has dwindled. As a news source, they are losing the ability to tell us what to think. The hypnotic hold that television advertising has had on our people is also eroding as the TV audience is shrinking. Voters are becoming freed from the electron tube.

We are similarly fed up with those who represent us in the decision-making councils of our nation. It has become clear that our congressmen and senators are so hopelessly dependent on special interests and their financial resources that we must doubt their ability to do what we want or need. Voters are determined to take as much direct control as possible of the decisions that affect their own lives. As we watch our politicians sell their votes for campaign contributions so they can afford to sell themselves to us through television, we are turning to the Internet to change the rules of the game.

By eliminating the high cost and lengthy delays that have always characterized communication among ordinary people living far apart, the Internet makes it possible to act upon our distrust of the media and politicians. The happy coincidence of the technical capacity for dialogue on the Net and the demand of voters to speak out and be heard have combined to trigger the rise of a new interactive replacement for the intermediaries of our current politics.

As direct democracy takes root, the American voter will become more involved and active. We don't have to wait anymore for the next election to express our views while Congress makes decisions for us. We don't have to wait on a call from a pollster to speak our piece. We are going to take to the Internet and tell our representatives what to do whenever we damn well feel like it.

In the first part of this book, we will explore the changes that Internet politics will bring. We will examine how direct popular referendums will increasingly take over the power of Congress and how political parties will lose what remains of their grip. We will probe why money will mean less in our politics than it ever has as political action moves from paid television to the free Internet.

Until now, all political campaigns shared one basic assumption— that political messages would be delivered to the voter without his or her consent. While watching our favorite television programs, we were assaulted by ads we did not request. They sold us beer, cars, and all manner of consumer goods. They also sold us politicians. They inflicted their messages on us whether we liked it or not. But in the Internet democracy, voters must ask for the messages. They must want to log on and click on a candidate's message. As the science of campaigning shifts its focus, all political dialogue will change.

It will be a brave new world.

·   ·   ·

Nowhere was the decline in the media's power more evident than during the central event of the late 1990s—the unimpeachment of President Bill Clinton. The second part of this book will examine how the members of the Fourth Estate have come to lose their power and pave the way for revolutionary change in our politics. By probing this most searing and revelatory political debate of recent history, we will see how far Americans have drifted from the days when they were happy to vest decision-making in the Fourth Estate. Indeed, Bill Clinton's presidency survived because he and his handlers realized that they were playing under new rules—the rules of the Fifth Estate.

Part One

HOW THE INTERNET
IS TAKING OVER

BY EARLY 1999, seventy-five million Americans over the age of sixteen were using the Internet, with 60 percent of them logging on every day. Internet use is growing by 25 percent per year. As everybody learns to log on, Internet voting will become the centerpiece of our democracy. While it will be many years before the politicians who control Congress and the state legislatures let us actually vote over the Internet, we Americans will use the Net anyway, increasingly and massively, to express our views to the government.

Chapter One

VOX POPULI IN CYBERSPACE

THOMAS JEFFERSON would have loved to see the Internet. His utopian vision of a democracy based on town meetings and direct popular participation is about to become a reality. In the era of the Fifth Estate, the massive, uncontrolled, and unregulated interaction of tens of millions of people will be the central political reality. Ideas, opinions, viewpoints, and perspectives will race back and forth over the Internet instantly and continuously, weaving together to create a new national fabric of democracy.

Input from a multiplicity of sources will make it impossible for any organization or agency to control the flow of information or the shaping of opinion. As Matt Drudge, the Internet investigative reporter, puts it, "Everybody will be a publisher, disseminating his views to all who choose to log on to read them." News organizations and opinion leaders will spring up all over in a wonderfully chaotic and anarchic freedom. Limitations imposed by capital, paper, and ink, or the unavailability of bands and frequencies, will no longer screen out the opinions of the less connected and less powerful.

Only a few years ago, the voting records of our elected officials were inaccessible, the identities of large campaign donors were obscured, and the expenditures by government and by campaigns were concealed by layers of bureaucracy. Only by joining one of the few public interest organizations, such as Public Interest Research Group (PIRG) or Common Cause, could we find some of this data. Even then, it was slow to reach us through monthly newsletters, annual reports, or pre-election mailings. All of that is in the past. Now we are able to get instantaneous and comprehensive reports of the activities of political figures. Through a wide array of documents placed on the Internet by organizations, individuals, and the press, we are inundated with the tools of effective citizenship.

The incredible speed and interactivity of the Internet will inevitably return our country to a de facto system of direct democracy by popular referendums. The town-meeting style of government will become a national reality. Eventually the 1990s contrived "town meetings" popularized by Bill Clinton will be obsolete, as voters will reject the idea of specially handpicked, agreeable participants who, in fact, don't reflect our towns. Instead, the real town meetings will occur on the Internet, with real people, and the politicians will have to listen.

Ad hoc, nonbinding voting over the Internet is starting to transform our democracy. A proliferation of political Web sites soon will offer voters the chance to be heard at the instant that an issue becomes important. Whether it is in response to a random act of violence such as Columbine, the death of an American icon like John F. Kennedy Jr., or a court decision such as O. J. Simpson's acquittal, American voters are already finding an outlet for their emotions and political views that has never before been available.

Through interactive political and news Web sites, people will be able to vote on any issue they wish. We will all be more like the citizens in California and other states where voters can take matters into their own hands through direct referendums and initiatives in each year's balloting. Internet referendums will not, in the beginning, have any legally binding effect, but they will be politically binding. As the number of people participating in these votes grows from the thousands well into the millions, they will acquire a political force that will compel our elected representatives, anxious to keep their jobs, to heed their message. No congressman, senator, or president would dare fly in the face of so massive an expression of public sentiment.

In all likelihood these Internet referendums will be staged without the slightest government participation. Private Web sites like Vote.com will provide the ballot boxes. Financed by advertising, these nongovernmental means of expressing voter opinion, in effect, mean the end of a government monopoly on the process of registration and voting.

When will voters be consulted on important issues? Whenever they want to be. Anytime enough Internet users want to have a referendum they will simply have one. There will likely be hundreds of referendums each year. Of course only a few will attract the attention of enough voters to matter politically, but, by the self-correcting increase or decrease in turnout, voters will indicate how important they feel a given issue to be. Some issues will arouse sufficient public attention to generate a huge outpouring of public opinion and tens of millions of votes. These referendums, on the key issues of the day, will have an enormous impact on governmental decision-making at all levels. Others will, undoubtedly, be flaky or unimportant. Then few will vote or participate and they will be ignored.

Elections will still be run by government bureaucracies. We'll still choose our president and Congress by the old election system, but the influence the public can bring to bear will make it far less important whom we elect. It is the public's will, not theirs, that will most often be controlling.

Is this a good thing? Our legislators and leaders, with their addiction to special-interest money and power, have forfeited their right to our trust. A little direct democracy might dilute the power of these self-interested and well-funded organizations and restore a measure of popular sovereignty. The insider system, with its focus on partisan combat and subservience to powerful lobbyists, could use a bit of fresh air now and then. Thomas Jefferson recommended a revolution every twenty years to "refresh . . . the tree of liberty." As revolutions go, this one is likely to be both more pacific and more constructive than most.

Of course voters make mistakes and are often turned from good sense by racism, bigotry, and prejudice. Demagogues make a good living off the gullible. Ultimately our experience with direct democracy will lead voters to see the wisdom of ceding back to those who are more experienced a measure of the power the Internet has given the general public. Eventually, chastened and humbled, our elected leaders may find the pendulum swinging back in their direction. But not anytime soon.

Whether direct Internet democracy is good or bad is, however, quite beside the point. It is inevitable. It is coming and we had better make our peace with it. We have to better educate ourselves so that we can make good decisions. Restricting the power of the people is no longer a viable option. The Internet made it obsolete.

People are yearning for some way to express their views on political issues, beyond talking back to an unresponsive television screen or muttering into their coffee over the morning newspaper. (As we shall see, this frustration with the limited opportunities for political self-expression is a basic reason for the popularity of talk radio's call-in format.)

How popular would Internet referendums become? An April 1999 survey by Dresner, Wickers and Associates, taken for the Vote.com Web site, predicts that upwards of 40 percent of people over sixteen years of age would be interested in participating.

The survey asked respondents on which issues they would like to vote. The answer is that significant numbers would like to vote on practically anything.

INTEREST IN VOTING ON THE INTERNET

Topic	% of Internet Users Who Are Interested		
	Very	Somewhat	Total
GENERAL INTEREST IN PARTICIPATING IN REFERENDUMS	25	19	44
. . . IN PRESIDENTIAL PRIMARIES	35	19	54
HOW SHOULD BUDGET SURPLUS BE SPENT?	48	20	68
SHOULD HILLARY RUN FOR THE SENATE?	20	9	29
SHOULD THE U.S. GRANT MORE TRADE CONCESSIONS TO CHINA?	20	14	34
SHOULD SALES OVER THE INTERNET BE TAXED?	24	12	36

(SOURCE: DRESNER, WICKERS AND ASSOCIATES SURVEY, APRIL 1999. 1,000 INTERNET USERS.)

How are we to reconcile this predicted quantum leap in voter interest with the depressing spectacle of annually dropping election-day turnout? While turnout has indeed decreased, the falloff is more illusory than real. As political consultant Richard Dresner puts it, the drop in voter turnout is "more a generational thing than anything else." Dresner notes that turnout among those reared during the Depression and amid World War II has always been very high, higher than that of any other generation. "Much of the drop in turnout," Dresner says, "is due to this generation dying out. Turnout among all other generations has been roughly the same over the past twenty or thirty years." The sole exception, he notes, is that there is a very low turnout among young adults who have not been to college.

As turnout drops, how will participation through the Internet rise? Will the X Generation, skilled in the Internet but indifferent to politics, remain online but continue to ignore the ballot box? Probably this is exactly what will happen.

Participation is a simple matter of logging on. There is no trip through the rain to the polling place. No authority-figure inspectors are there to look up your name in the Doomsday Book to verify your status as a legal voter.

Internet users may not elect public officials, but they will tell those officials what to do. Indeed, referendum voting over the Internet will likely become as habitual as reading a newspaper or using e-mail. Instantly the voter will see his or her vote counted and can log on to follow the progress of the referendum. Those who vote will soon learn how their representative in Congress, the state legislature, or the city council voted on the issue at hand. Feedback will be instantaneous and responsive.

Will the resulting vote-count truly mirror the opinions of those who will really vote to select their senators and congressmen on election day? At first, probably not. But in a society where only about half of voting-age adults actually participates in presidential elections, and only about 40 percent in off-year congressional contests, why should this national canvass of opinion exclude the other half to two-thirds? Indeed, as nonvoters get used to voting over the Internet, they will find themselves more involved in the political process and may well become interested enough to make the journey to the polls on election day.

. . .

Internet use is disproportionately concentrated among those under fifty, but contrary to popular wisdom, its use among minorities is extensive. While the proportion of Internet users who are Black or Hispanic is somewhat less than that of the general population, it does approximate their proportion of those who actually vote. The following table compares the proportion of Internet users from each age and race group with their percentage of the general population.

INTERNET USE BY AGE AND RACE

Age or Racial Group	% of Net Users	% of Population over 16
16–30	39	27
31–50	46	40
51–65	11	17
OVER 65	4	16
BLACK	11	12
HISPANIC	5	11

Only Hispanics and those over sixty-five are grossly under-represented on the Internet. The former is likely due, in part, to linguistic problems, which will be overcome as the years pass. As Internet use grows, the participation of Americans over sixty-five is certain to increase. The Internet population is more and more likely to be a reflection of America.

Obviously, a fair number of people under the age of eighteen will also vote in Internet referendums. While these young people would not be able to vote in actual elections, they will likely still want to use the Internet to send messages to the adult leadership of their country. As teen habits go, voting is relatively less pernicious than smoking, drinking, or drug use, so why not encourage it? The Internet will redefine citizenship.

Will Internet voting be subject to fraud or abuse? Technology can, or soon will, likely be able to stop multiple voting. Every once in a while, a dedicated hacker will be up to the challenge of invading the system and recording multiple votes, but systems can be put in place to prevent any substantial abuse of the process. The validity of an Internet referendum will depend mainly on the verification system of the Web site.

As Internet voting becomes widespread and the turnout for Internet referendums mounts, the energies of our political system will flow into the Internet and further increase its impact. Candidates will campaign over the Internet. Lobbying groups will use Internet voting to animate their positions. Special-interest organizations will adapt themselves to using Internet referendums to make their political points. A new arena will be created that will absorb more and more of the kinetic energy of our political process.

•   •   •

Now let's take a look at how the era of the Internet voters, the Fifth Estate, will affect the players in our politics.

Chapter Two

THE INCREDIBLE
SHRINKING CONGRESS

AS THE POWER of the Fourth Estate fades and the influence of spokespersons, spin doctors, and news analysts declines, no one will feel the loss of authority more than our elected officials. The middlemen in our political process protected officeholders.

In the new era, Congress will have to listen to us. When we cast our votes, our opinions will be instantly conveyed to our congressmen and senators, and they will feel us breathing down their necks as they vote.

While voters tend to track closely the actions of their president, governor, and mayor, those with legislative as opposed to executive authority tend to escape close public scrutiny. Congress casts over six hundred votes each year. An issue that sparks controversy, such as gun control, will likely be voted on, in one form or another, fifty or sixty times. Even the most conscientious of voters would find it an almost impossible task to keep track of the votes his congressman or senator casts. With a typical legislative session lasting about one hundred and fifty or so days, the average member casts upwards of four votes each day. It would be a full-time job for any voter to keep close tabs on each one.

Even were we all to monitor the votes of our representatives with the requisite intensity, we would still end up befuddled. Without a scorecard, it is almost impossible to make sense of the various procedural motions and counterproposals on which congressmen vote each day. A measure that might seem to be pro gun control might actually be a weaker substitute proposed by the NRA in the hope of muddling the issue.

As a result, most of our information about how our congressman or senator votes comes from advertising by his opponent around election time. It is then, and only then, that we hear the bad news about the decisions he has made with which we disagree. We need to rely on the give-and-take of political dialogue to enlighten us before we vote.

The impotence we feel in the current environment would provoke the empathy of our great-grandparents. Originally, United States senators were elected by their state legislatures, not by the voters directly. When Lincoln debated Douglas in their famous 1858 race for the Senate, they never actually appeared against one another on the ballot. They were contesting seats in the Illinois state legislature whose members then decided whether to reelect Douglas or replace him with Lincoln. (Lincoln won more seats than Douglas did, but there were so many Democrats whose seats were not up for election that year that Douglas held on to a majority in the legislature and retained his seat in the Senate.)

By the Progressive Era of the late nineteenth and early twentieth centuries, public anger at the special-interest domination of the Senate began to mount. Tom Nast, a political cartoonist, depicted the U.S. Senate as populated by puppets who danced while their strings were pulled by special interests and monopolistic trusts. To open the Senate to the will of the people, progressives led by President Woodrow Wilson passed the Seventeenth Amendment to the Constitution in 1913 requiring direct election of senators.

Today, public anger at the increasing domination of both houses of Congress by campaign contributions from special interests has again reached a boil. As the cost of campaigning escalates, voters understand that those who fund the candidacies of senators and congressmen usually get to dominate their thinking and their voting. Once again, the public is demanding reform.

But the powers that control Congress will never allow campaign finance reform. Elected under the current corrupt system, these incumbents use the financial advantage that special-interest money gives them to defeat their opponents and stay in office. They are against any change.

The political parties are equally phony on the issue of campaign finance reform. When Democrats controlled both houses of Congress and the presidency from 1993 to 1994, they forgot all about reforming the campaign finance system. When President

Clinton tried to push them, Democratic congressional leaders advised him to downplay the issue and he did. It was not until the Republicans took control of Congress in 1995 that the Democrats decided to back reform. Then, supremely confident that the GOP would reject any real change in campaign finance laws, they unstintingly advocated it. Knowing reform would never pass, they saw no danger in backing it.

For their part, Republicans know that reform might mean the end of their control of Congress. The representatives of the wealthy GOP candidates always outspend their Democratic rivals. Even as formidable a fundraiser as Bill Clinton had to compete with his Republican opponent, Bob Dole, in 1996 with only half as much money as the GOP had.

The American people, in their demand for reform, are not to be denied. They will not take to the streets, they will just log on and use the Internet to instruct their representatives on how to vote.

For members of the Fifth Estate, every issue of consequence that comes before Congress will simultaneously go on the Internet for public consultation. Long before the congressmen and senators cast their yea or nay votes in their hallowed legislative halls, millions of regular, ordinary people will have cast theirs on the Internet. By the time of the actual vote in Congress, each member will get a printout of how tens or hundreds of thousands of people in his or her district or state voted on the issue. When the senator from California learns that her constituents, by a margin of four million to three million, have voted against Fast Track trade legislation, you can bet that she will vote no as well. As Senator Everett Dirksen of Illinois once said, "When they feel the heat, they see the light."

Although still in their infancy, Vote.com and similar Web sites offer the very real possibility of becoming a decisive force in influencing national decision-making. Today congressional vote-counters routinely calculate the "presidential support score" of each member, indicating the percentage of the time the representative or senator supported the president's position. Other support scores show the proportion of the time the member voted for or against his own party. Each major interest group issues annual report cards rating how often each congressman backed the group's position on pending legislation.

In the future, congressmen and senators will get a "people's support score" indicating how often he agreed with the majority of his voters who expressed their views over the Internet. No longer will voters have to hunt through the newspaper to catch a glimpse, buried in an inside page, of how members of Congress from their area voted. Instead, those who participate in the Internet voting will instantly learn whether their representative agreed or disagreed with their position.

Although polls already have a decisive influence over how Congress votes, the Internet referendums will dwarf their impact. In a poll, the public is passive. Only those who are actually sampled know that they have been surveyed. The rest of us just read the results. We may agree with the poll's conclusion, but nobody asked us what we think. We have only read what the laws of statistics say we think.

These days we are conditioned to think in percentages. We learn that 48 percent of Americans feel one way and 43 percent feel the other way about an issue before our country. In the Internet referendums, percentages will matter less than raw numbers. The more important the question, the more deeply held our views, the more people will log on and vote. If a referendum attracts only a few hundred thousand votes throughout the nation, it will have little impact regardless of the results. But if millions log on and participate, an enormous political force has come into being—the clearly expressed will of a large number of people.

Internet referendums and e-mail to congressmen will overshadow the methods we currently have of expressing our views to those who represent us. A congressman who gets a few hundred letters on an issue usually feels that he is watching a massive groundswell of public opinion. A few hundred phone calls is usually enough to make his switchboard seem under siege. But through the Internet he will soon get huge numbers of e-mails and will have to take account of the expressed opinions of tens of thousands in his district. He will have to listen.

Will a dedicated group of special-interest pleaders be able to overwhelm such Internet referendums and mask the fact that their views are still in the minority? It is doubtless that most will try, and try hard. Some may generate the millions of Internet votes needed to create such an impression, but the energies of the political dialogue will soon animate those on the other side and their greater numbers will bring the results closer to reality.

What if the only people who care enough to log on and to vote are of a certain persuasion and the rest of us don't really give a damn? Then they will carry the day—and they should. After all, our government needs to pay attention not just to the will of the majority of our people, but also to the opinions of those who care most deeply. Intensity of feeling, as well as numerical superiority, must factor into the equation of popular will. Intensity has always been a factor in regular elections.

This erosion of "leadership" and the growth of democracy will be deeply disturbing to many. Many accuse political figures like President Clinton of "governing by polls," an ironic accusation in a democracy where leaders are supposed to be responsive to the views of those who elect them. The attack exposes a vital tension and balance in our system of government between direct democracy and representative government. Those we elect are supposed to lead *and* to listen. They need to keep one finger pointed in the direction in which they would lead us and another finger on the pulse of the public. But as our faith in the independence and goodwill of those we elect has declined, we have been less willing to let them lead and more insistent that they listen to us.

· · ·

Voters have been taking matters into their own hands since the 1970s, in the aftermath of Vietnam and Watergate. Increasingly they have seen congressmen and senators as representing the special interests who financed their campaigns, not the common good.

We scrutinize the voting records of our congressmen and senators as never before. Challengers run negative ads attacking the incumbent's vote on pivotal issues like abortion, school prayer, tax cuts, welfare reform, and anticrime legislation. Congressmen and senators, for their parts, deliberately have forced recorded votes on controversial amendments in the hope of building a case for the ouster of incumbents of the other party.

Where once the Congress ruled by consensus, burying disagreements between the parties in compromises and unrecorded committee votes, now on-the-record floor votes have become the norm, creating a record that was thoroughly exposed and debated during election campaigns.

In the '80s, special-interest groups revised their lobbying methods to take into account the increased public desire for participation in the decisions that affected their lives. Where once lobbying was a matter of quietly buttonholing a senator here or a congressman there at diplomatic receptions and dinner parties, now it became more about influencing the public in the hope that they would sway their legislators. Lobbying used to be directed upward—at legislators. Now it is frequently directed downward—at getting ordinary people to e-mail, write, or phone their representatives to urge them to heed their wishes. Lobbying has gone grass roots.

In particularly contested battles—as when liberals sought to stop the confirmation of Reagan Supreme Court nominee

Robert Bork—advocates actually began to run advertisements on radio and television to move public opinion. This direct communication with the voters on crucial issues reached new heights when the health insurance industry battled successfully against Hillary Clinton's healthcare-reform program by running very effective advertisements. A fictional couple, Harry and Louise, sat at the kitchen table discussing the healthcare proposals. Harry convinced Louise and much of America that the Clinton plan would eliminate the voluntary choice of doctors and impair health care. Learning from that example, when the antitobacco movement sought to pass legislation raising cigarette taxes and regulating tobacco advertising aimed at teenagers, the industry took to the airwaves to stimulate opposition to the proposals.

Terrified by the intrusion of the voter into the once-insulated clubby world of Congress, politicians have come to follow the polls, reducing the leadership and increasing followership among our elected officials. As polls have become more frequent and more detailed, they have offered leaders such pinpoint assessments of public opinion that they often inhibit the timid from speaking out for bold new programs and proposals.

In short, balance in our system has already begun its swing toward direct democracy and away from representative democracy. Our representatives had our trust and they blew it. Along with all the intermediates of the Fourth Estate, their power is dropping. With the rise of Internet voting by the Fifth Estate, the pendulum will continue to swing toward direct popular control.

Just as Jefferson predicted, increasing educational and informational levels have played a major part in increasing the demand for more popular control of the day-to-day decision-making of our government. In the words of James Harrington, "The wisdom of the few may be the light of mankind; but the interest of the few is not the profit of mankind."

This change is inevitable. The question is whether we can make it desirable. If we concentrate on educating our people well, they can use this new power wisely.

In the long run, Internet voting will not only make Congress more responsive to popular will, but it will also make it a lot less desirable place to be. Already the pressures of fundraising, limitations on outside income, and the scrutiny of negative advertising provoke retirements each year. But as the public uses the Net to look over the shoulders of their representatives and pry more deeply into the affairs of Congress, more senators and congressmen than ever are likely to look for new careers.

The job of senator or congressman will no longer seem as exalted as it does today, perhaps opening the way for more average people—and fewer millionaires—to apply for the job. Just as the office of the presidency has lost the trappings of the increasingly imperial status it had achieved, so the office of congressman and senator will be diminished. Voters have tried to achieve the same end by imposing term limits on their legislators. The Internet will prove a much more effective way to bring our elected representatives back to earth.

Chapter Three

VIRTUAL ELECTIONS

IN TIME, the Internet will replace the voting machine. It will become the ballot box. But the politicians won't let it happen anytime soon. They fear the higher turnout that home Internet voting would bring. A lot of elected officials who piously bemoan low turnouts fear higher ones, knowing they could be thrown out of their jobs. They will do their best to preserve the traditional way of voting—behind a curtain in a school or fire station. Lawmakers will resist Internet voting just as they fought to block motor-voter legislation, which allows people to register to vote when they get their drivers' licenses.

Their argument will be that Internet balloting will permit unqualified voters to participate in the election. Eventually, however, the Internet should be able to screen unregistered noncitizens and underaged voters from participation. Already Republicans in Louisiana have contracted with an Internet voting firm to permit party members to vote through the Internet in that state's presidential nominating caucuses in 2000.

Long before the actual franchise is exercised over the Internet, the ad hoc development of informal Internet voting will come to dominate the nominating and electoral process. As it is now, the few hundred thousand who vote in the early contests have a disproportionate influence on the nominating process. Iowa's caucuses have an impact on the New Hampshire primary, which in turn influences the votes in the Super Tuesday primaries throughout the South. Now the Internet primary will be the first domino to fall. Already the Vote.com Web site has announced its intention to hold a presidential primary on the Internet. With aggressive marketing, it is possible that millions will vote online to help choose the nominees of both parties.

The Internet primary will provide the first real measure of a candidate's national strength. The small number of delegates at stake in the New Hampshire primary and the Iowa caucuses matters little. But as tests of strength, they loom large. So it will be with the Internet primary. As pundits and prognosticators ponder the early signs to discern trends and handicap the presidential race, Internet voting will be the bellwether of a candidate's appeal and electability. If candidates fare well on the Internet, their campaigns can take off. If they fall below expectations, it may be a precursor of their demise.

Candidates seeking to jump-start their own candidacies will use the Internet to acquire momentum. One early indication of how they will use the Internet was Steve Forbes's announcement of his presidential candidacy for 2000 over his own Web site. Increasingly, candidates will devote their energies, organizations, and funds to catalyzing participation in the Internet primary. They will work overtime to get out the vote. Faced with strong challenges from second-rank candidates, the front-runners will have to plunge in and make a good showing.

In the 1988 race for the Republican nomination for president, Bush manager Lee Atwater perfected a strategy of using ad hoc events to demonstrate Bush's dominance over Dole in the early running. When Michigan announced a party conclave months before any state held its primary, Atwater worked hard to win the straw poll for his candidate. By assigning importance to these nonbinding beauty contests among the party faithful, Atwater was able to convey a sense of legitimacy and even inevitability to the Bush candidacy.

Similarly, in the 2000 race for the Republican presidential nomination, the August 1999 picnic of twenty-five thousand party faithful in Iowa assumed tremendous importance. If a few thousand party members gathered at a picnic can help sift through the contenders in the early going during the long road to the nomination, imagine what millions voting on the Internet could do.

There may well be Internet presidential debates as the various candidates find it necessary to pay obeisance to the power of the new medium by participating in an online test of their rhetorical ability. And soon candidates will advertise on the Internet-primary

Web site in the hope of reaching directly those who are about to sit in judgment on their candidacies.

. . .

As trial heats over the Internet become significant in the nominating process, their impact will spread to the state and local levels. When men and women want to float their candidacies for Senate, Congress, or governorship, they will find that they must compete in ad hoc Internet referendums to prove their viability. A strong early showing in the Internet voting could mean millions in campaign contributions. Just as published polls in statewide races designate the front-runner and establish a pecking order before the campaign has even started, Internet voting will play a huge role in deciding who potential supporters and financial donors think can win.

During election campaigns, when the candidates have already been nominated and face each other directly in electoral competition, Internet voting will usurp the role now played by political polling. Not only will the comparative Internet vote totals among the candidates help to establish who has momentum and who is fading, but the activism denoted by a candidate's ability to amass significant online support will also make him an appealing option.

As developments unfold in an election campaign, voters will express their reactions through Internet voting. When candidates make mistakes or face each other in debates, the Internet results will provide a national tracking poll far more profound than the spin propounded by handlers and advocates.

In times gone by, candidates would stage torchlight parades and large rallies. Television has anesthetized the political process and all we get are statistics instead of drama to show the strength of the candidates. But the Internet will restore life to the process. As more and more people log on to support an incipient candidacy, the mounting totals will reveal an enthusiasm and a commitment that will help generate further momentum.

Candidates running for president have to trudge through the snows of New Hampshire to demonstrate their seriousness and to pay homage to the state's traditional role as the first primary in the nation. Seeking the support of the Fifth Estate, candidates will go online to chat with voters. They will pose for pictures at their keyboards as often as they show up at donut shops in the primary states.

Internet primaries and Internet voting in elections will change how we choose our candidates, making them appeal to a national audience at the start of their candidacies. It will make the process of nomination and election an active one—an interactive one—and will stimulate voters to new levels of involvement and participation. It will be a healthy shot in the arm for a democracy increasingly devoid of passion.

Chapter Four

THE DIMINISHING IMPORTANCE
OF MONEY IN ELECTIONS

THE COST OF CAMPAIGNS began to rise geometrically when television advertising came to dominate elections. Before television, campaigns didn't cost nearly what they do today. Recently the cost of elections has soared even higher because of the shrinkage of the TV audience. So many are using the Internet, their VCRs, or watching cable television stations that do not accept advertising that, as fewer people are watching broadcast television, it is taking more money and more ads to reach the same number of voters. Campaigns now have to run ads twice as often as they once did in order to have the same impact. As a result, the cost of these ads is twice as high. These trends will continue, to the detriment of advertisers.

Currently, the costs of political campaigns seem to soar even higher with each election. In the early going of the 2000 election,

Governor George W. Bush Jr. was credited with a lead because he had amassed the princely sum of $37 million while Gore had raised only $17 million by the June 1999 filing.

This continuing and increasing importance of money in the 2000 election is the last gasp of the law of diminishing returns. With no other way to reach voters and no experience of Internet campaigning, politicians respond to the decrease in the television audience by merely increasing the amount they spend on television advertising. More and more money will be spent on swaying elections as money becomes less and less effective.

But when the percentage of the American public watching prime-time network television drops even further, and the percentage of households that are online during prime viewing hours increases, buying television time will no longer be an effective way to reach voters. When that tipping point comes—likely by the 2008 election—money will lose most of its power in our politics.

As Internet use increases, it will trigger a pronounced cut in the concentration of voters watching or listening to any given program on television or reading any particular newspaper. Density is the key to effective advertising. Only if voters are easily accessible through a limited number of outlets does it pay to go after them with ads.

Until the '80s, most voters dutifully clustered around the television set at night. They all watched one of the network news shows and then switched to their favorite prime-time programs. Later they turned on the local news. Their habits were predictable and they were easy to reach with ads. If you bought advertising on these programs, you got voters' attention.

In the '90s, viewing habits have become much more diversified. Many people watch movies on video at night. Forty-two percent of those who watch television in prime time are tuned in to cable stations, many of which do not air ads at all. Independent broadcast stations further increase the choices available. As more households install satellite dishes, they have even more choices of stations and programs to watch. More and more people are logging on to the Internet at night rather than turning on their television sets at all. Some voters still even venture out-of-doors in the evenings.

When half or more of the households are on the Net each evening and the rest are divided among hundreds of TV stations, who will find it financially attractive to buy television ads? Commercial advertisers, whose ad budgets dwarf those of political campaigns, will likely continue to use the airwaves. For them, decreased media density just means that it takes longer to reach the potential market, but television will still be useful in targeting specific groups of consumers. For those who only want to increase their market share by a few percentage points, or who want to aim their ads at certain demographic groups, TV broadcast advertising will still work.

Political campaigns do not have enough flexibility to adapt to these changes. Their budgets are sharply limited. They do not have months and months to make their case, reaching a limited number of viewers each night in the hope of hitting them all in the long run. Their election calendars are unforgiving and have a definite end on election day. Political advertisers need to reach vast numbers of people—usually a majority of the voters, to be exact. They can't afford to spend their resources on boutique advertising aimed at demographic subgroups.

Already the decreasing power of money in politics is becoming apparent. In the 1996 election, Republican nominee Bob Dole outspent President Clinton by two to one, but was badly defeated. In 1998, Senator Alfonse D'Amato in New York State spent more than challenger Chuck Schumer, but Schumer won. In California, Al Checci, co-chairman of Northwest Airlines, spent $35 million of his own money, but lost the Democratic primary to Lieutenant Governor Gray Davis, who professed to have "experience money can't buy." Meanwhile, in California's Republican primary, Jane Harman spent $20 million from her own fortune and still didn't win a seat in the Senate.

But for now, money still talks very loudly in politics. Most observers have assumed that the trend will continue until Congress enacts tougher campaign finance reforms. But they are wrong. We are seeing the final gasp of money in politics. It has become increasingly expensive to get elected, because television advertising is more expensive and less effective than it has ever been. If current trends continue, the broadcast television networks will attract less than a quarter of the prime-time audience by 2010, if not sooner.

As television advertising becomes less effective for political campaigns, candidates will find that they have to go where the voters are—to the Internet.

.   .   .

Internet advertising is still in its earliest stages. The first campaign ads were placed on the Internet only two years ago. In 1998 the total of all Internet advertising was $1.9 billion, an increase of 34 percent over the previous year. Even at this early stage, Internet advertising has now passed outdoor billboard advertising in revenue. Whether the Internet will prove to be a good advertising medium through which to reach voters will remain unclear for several years.

These days, Internet advertising is not very expensive. Advertisers pay from $5 to $30 on average for every thousand visitors to the Web site who see their ad. Each page of a Web site can feature one or more ads, usually run as banners. To click or not to click, that is the question for each viewer—but the advertiser pays whether they click or not. Relatively inexpensive, this means that a candidate whose banner is seen by a million voters would only have to pay about $10,000 for the privilege.

Will Internet advertising costs escalate, as have the costs on radio and television? Will the hope that Internet campaigning will reduce the role of money in politics prove evanescent? Obviously, the more demand there is for Internet advertising, the more expensive it will become. Yet the increased demand is not likely to ever drive prices as high as broadcast or cable media advertising. The supply of Internet advertising space is simply too vast, too unregulated, and expanding too quickly to allow demand to drive the prices up rapidly. While a few well-used Web sites can charge top dollar to advertisers, there will always be new Web sites with a new audience that will attract large numbers of visitors. This pluralism, unrestricted by a bandwidth like those on radio or television frequencies, will keep the costs of Internet advertising within reach for the foreseeable future.

That the Internet is a good way to get news information to voters is evident. In 1999 more than twenty million adults used the Internet as a daily source of news.

Thus, as the power of money declines, the importance of making news and getting communications out on the Net will increase. The candidate who has something to say and can generate interesting copy day in and day out will have an advantage over those who are simply buying their way onto the airwaves through ads.

The Internet also offers voters access to news information from myriad sources. One can find the *New York Times* and the Drudge Report and everything else in between. This pluralism increases the possibility of verifying reports; it encourages critical thinking. Voters will feel less manipulated when they read the news. No longer will they feel spoon-fed the priorities and opinions of their local newspaper or TV station. Only the most hardened of political junkies can even begin to subscribe to the vast number of periodicals easily available on the Net. Most of us subscribe to our local newspaper and a few magazines. Through the

Net, we can tap into a vast range of magazines, news services, newspapers, newsletters, and news-oriented Web sites—for free.

The proliferation of news on the Internet, and the decreasing power of paid advertising, will create a new dynamic in political funding. Candidates who raise vast amounts of money from special-interest groups will find themselves on the defensive. Their dollars will reach fewer people over the airwaves and the political problems caused by raising the money from special interests will dwarf the potential benefit as voters examine, online, who is giving money to whom. Each special-interest campaign contribution will become an issue. If a candidate takes money from utilities, polluters, trial lawyers, the NRA, labor unions, or other unpopular special interests, he will pay for it among the voters. The Internet will police campaign contributions by reporting to voters on who is funding which candidate.

Today the sources of campaign funds loom less large as issues because nobody is pure. Everybody needs to raise as much money as he can as quickly as he can. Rare is the candidate whose list of donors would not turn off voters were it adequately publicized. Candidates who want to make an issue of their virtue by refusing special-interest money are caught in a Catch-22 because they cannot raise enough money to publicize the fact that they aren't taking special-interest money.

As money means less and less, more candidates will find it in their best political interest to be very selective in their fundraising. If television advertising is no longer a great way to reach voters, why buy yourself a negative campaign issue by raising funds from unsavory sources? Campaign fundraisers will find that they must be much more careful about how and from whom they take contributions.

While all of these influences will combine to make money less important than it has been in political campaigns, this is only half the story. As the power of Congress itself decreases, as voters make more decisions themselves by voting on issues online, fewer private citizens or lobbyists will be lining up at the doors of campaign officials with checks to influence candidates.

With Internet voting usurping much of the power now vested in Congress, a special-interest group would be better served to spend its money influencing us—the voters—than influencing them—the politicians.

As Congress and the state legislatures become more like rubber stamps for our will—as we express it through Internet voting—industry and trade associations will be less willing to donate large amounts to candidates or even to incumbents, further decreasing the role of money in elections.

The Congress will never allow real campaign finance reform to pass. Those who serve in elective office got there under the current rules. For the most part, it was their ability to raise money that permitted them to win. The last thing they want to do is to share this advantage with insurgents. On this issue, both parties are united, but they play a game in which the party in power kills reform while the party that can't pass it advocates it. When the

Democrats ran Congress, campaign finance reform never saw the light of day. But when the GOP took over, the same party that had bottled up reform measures and had begged Clinton not to push them suddenly became passionate devotees of reform, now that they were sure they wouldn't succeed.

It is becoming a dead issue. The natural forces of change in the media, the Internet, and our politics are going to make financial power less and less effective, more politically costly, and less available to American politicians.

Thank goodness.

.   .   .

As the Internet lures voters away from their television sets and limits the importance of money in elections, the political money-changers in the temple—the fundraisers and the fat-cat donors—will lose their hallowed seats. Now the kings and queens of the political process, their disproportionate influence is felt at all levels of the political process. But as their money buys ads on TV programs that fewer and fewer people are watching, and the Internet becomes the main vehicle for political communications, money won't buy political happiness. It is too late. The power is already in the hands of the members of the Fifth Estate. And they are online.

Can these power brokers maintain their influence with the Fifth Estate? It's not very likely. As hard as it is to imagine a day when fundraising does not consume 70 percent of a candidate's day, the time is coming . . . and soon.

Chapter Five

THE NEW VOTERS—
THE X GENERATION ASSERTS
ITS POWER

THE MOST ALIENATED age group in our society is young voters. They are known as the X Generation. Turnout among those under thrity-five is the lowest of any age group and is dropping the fastest. The Internet is their organ, their window to the world. So minimal has been their imprint on our society that Americans under the age of thirty-five don't even have the dignity of a real name attached to their generation. Those who came of age in the Roaring Twenties are called the Lost Generation. The young adults of the '30s and '40s are honored as the GI Generation. Their children, who reached adulthood in the '50s, are the Silent Generation. Then come the Boomers and finally the X Generation. Even their children have a name, the Millennium Generation, but they remain denoted only by the letter X.

During Clinton's unimpeachment, the X generation had its first moment on center stage. It saved the Clinton presidency. As campaigns move from one-way involuntary propaganda to two-way interactive dialogue, we have a wonderful opportunity to bring back into the process many of these turned-off voters who have moved away from any active participation. The excitement, stimulation, interactivity, and sheer fun of the Internet dialogue will stimulate many to develop political consciousness.

The irony of American politics is that the people who are most tuned in to new technologies, the Internet, and computers in general are the least likely to vote on election day. Far from inert or deadened, these nonvoters lead lively lives e-mailing back and forth. They are not dropouts. They live in their own world on the Internet and pay little attention to the traditional organs of politics—newspapers and television news programs.

But as politics comes to the Internet, it will also come to these young voters. It will come into their homes in a way it has never done before. They won't have to leave the high-tech world and enter the universe of "snail mail," boring television, and newspapers in order to speak out and be heard. A generation of mouse-clickers will not have to become page-turners in order to participate in politics.

In 1996, while 49 percent of all voting-age Americans voted, only 39 percent of those eighteen to thirty-five did so. The following table gives details:

1996 VOTER TURNOUT BY AGE

Age Group	% of Voting-Age Adults Who Voted
18–20	31
21–24	33
25–34	43
35–44	55
45–64	62*
OVER 65	63*

*ESTIMATED

The situation is getting worse and worse. In the past twenty years, turnout among the young has dropped sharply.

1980–1996 TURNOUT OF VOTERS UNDER 35

Year	% of Under-35 Population That Voted
1980	49
1988	42
1992	48
1996	39

Ironically, it is these voters under thirty-five who are the main users of the Internet. While they represent only 27 percent of the population, they account for 39 percent of Internet users. There is no better way to reach this alienated group of young Americans.

If Internet use among young voters is extraordinarily high, it is even larger among those too young to vote. Internet campaigning may be the crucial force in rekindling a thirst for democratic participation among those who will soon join the electorate. By relying on polls to remain in office, Bill Clinton effectively enfranchised a generation of voters who hadn't taken the trouble to go to the ballot box. Indeed, once politics comes to the Internet, we may well find that the youngest voters are the ones who turn out in the greatest numbers.

This change in the demographics of the electorate will send shock waves through the political system. As we have seen, the X Generation showed its political power and homogeneity during the unimpeachment process. For the first time in American politics, the under-thirty-five-year-old voter held the key to the president's fate. The lamb roared.

· · ·

The Xers came of age after the Boomer Generation had picked things clean. William Strauss and Neil Howe, in their book *Generations,* a classic study, liken the X Generation's experience in growing up to ". . . coming to a beach at the very end of a long summer of big crowds and wild goings-on. The beach bunch is sunburned, the sand shopworn, hot, and full of debris. . . . That's how [the X Generation] feels following the Boomers."

Strauss and Howe go on to describe very well the priorities of the Xers:

They look upon themselves as pragmatic, quick, sharp-eyed, able to step outside themselves to understand the game of life as it really gets played. . . . [They] see no welcome mat on their economic future. . . . Money isn't everything but . . . money means survival, and for a generation whose earliest life experiences taught them not to trust others, survival must come first.

Their survival instincts are well-honed and pragmatism dominates their thinking. Causes, movements, political theories were for their more fortunate parents. For them, there has been only the search for a good-paying job, a stable family life, and a place to live. Often the product of broken homes, the X Generation came to value family and stability more than their footloose parents did.

Politically, Ronald Reagan was their savior. His infectious personality dispelled the pessimism of Jimmy Carter. As Reagan brought taxes down and moved the economy up, the X Generation found survival a bit easier. Though Boomers welcomed the narcissism of the Reagan years and joined its headlong rush to hedonism, the self-involvement of the Xers was about assuring their new families the basics of survival.

Their love affair with the GOP came to a sharp halt during the recession of 1991. These vulnerable young people found their jobs lost or in peril and their tenuous hold on a middle-class existence under assault. As President Bush seemed to dally in the face of an economic downturn, they turned to the newcomer, Bill Clinton, for relief. Abandoning their Republicanism, they voted for Clinton by nine points in the 1992 election.

But their enthusiasm for Clinton was distinctly limited. He seemed the quintessential Baby Boomer adult: hedonistic, self-indulgent, and promiscuous. This drug-using, draft-dodging president did not play well among the hard-working, down-to-earth X Generation.

Strauss and Howe note that for the X Generation "the symbolic meanings—of sex, drugs, student rights, whatever—had all failed. What they found, instead, were the harsh realities of social pathology. One by one they have slowed or reversed these trends—the SAT decline, the youth crime, the substance abuse, the early sex. . . ."

In their own lives, the X Generation, impelled by pragmatism and realism, walked the straight and narrow. Morality was important to them. Having witnessed their parents' excesses, they "just said no" to drugs, resisted the lure of the sexual revolution, and cut back on drunk driving. Teen pregnancy rates began to drop (down 6 percent since 1994), drug use plummeted, and DUI deaths were down. The X Generation married later and divorced less often than their Boomer parents had. Once they married, they had children. Birth rates, anemic through the '60s and '70s, soared in the late '80s and '90s as the X Generation started its families. Even single fathers began to face their responsibilities. In 1998, 1.5 million identified themselves, compared with only a third of that number in 1992. More religious than their parents, 45 percent of the X

Generation attends church at least once a week, compared with only 34 percent of Americans thirty-six to fifty-five years of age.

Increasingly, the X Generation became estranged from Bill Clinton. In 1995, Clinton's polling showed that his biggest losses had come from among young parents. While he was carrying single people and breaking even among those who were married but did not have children living at home, he was losing badly among parents with live-in kids.

Surveying the wreckage of his presidency after losing control of Congress to the Republicans in 1994, Clinton, brilliantly seizing the initiative, set out to win the hearts of America's young parents. One by one, he laid out the pieces of a sweeping agenda to address their every need.

He helped them get time off from work to bond with their newborn babies by passing the Family Leave Law.

He made childhood immunization universal, inoculating children against disease and effectively inoculating their parents against Republican attacks on his administration.

As their children came of preschool age, Clinton doubled the Head Start program so that it could accommodate all the children whose parents wanted it.

Were the schools swollen with the children of the new baby boom? Clinton fought for funds to build new schools and renovate old ones.

Were classes too large? The president battled for 100,000 extra teachers, paid for with federal funding.

Concerned about school standards? Clinton pushed for uniform national testing.

Worried about increased property taxes to finance schools? Clinton battled Republicans to expand federal help for education.

As their children grew older, X Generation parents worried more about issues like values, crime, and violence. Clinton faced down the TV networks and made them implement a ratings system. Meanwhile, he got Congress to pass legislation requiring the installation of a V-chip in each new television set. Thanks to this technology, parents could keep sex and violence off their television sets. To cut crime, Clinton got funds for 100,000 extra police and more money for drug counselors in schools. His controls on handguns let many parents breathe easier as crime rates dropped. To protect younger children, he pushed Congress to require safety locks on guns.

As parents worried about discipline, Clinton advocated tougher truancy enforcement, school uniforms, and teenage curfews.

When their children were ready for college, the X Generation appreciated Clinton's efforts to cut interest rates on student loans, expand Pell scholarship grants, and initiate HOPE scholarships, which paid the full tuition costs at most two-year public community colleges.

Everywhere parents turned, there was Clinton with a program to meet their needs. All of them had social utility. The Boomers who controlled the media derided the Clinton initiatives, calling them "small bore" and lacking in vision. They asked how issues like school uniforms and teen curfews could compare with the great themes of the past—the New Deal, the New Frontier, and the Great Society.

But these media critics missed the essential point. Clinton had recognized what they had not—that the opinions and values of Generation X could be used to put pressure on Congress. The power structure of the Fourth Estate was Boomers or older, unaccustomed to granting these kids a place at the table. Never before had the views of the quiet, timid, self-involved Xers much mattered.

Clinton realized that they felt surrounded on all sides by sex and violence while trying to raise children with values and a sense of decency. They had no time for political theory. They wanted help in the day-to-day tasks of parenting. And Clinton met their needs.

. . .

The Republicans did not. Insisting that education remain a state and local issue, they missed the point and missed the boat. Parents knew how fundamentally the world was changing and how poorly their schools were keeping pace. More and more they noticed the dichotomy between their computer-dominated homes (44 percent of all American homes have computers) and the blackboard-dominated classrooms their children returned to each morning. At home, their kids logged on, played computer games, e-mailed their friends, and visited chat rooms at night. But from nine to three it was a different world. Taught by men and women who did not know about computers, in schools that lacked access to the Internet, it was as if the school bus had become a time machine transporting children back ten years to a precomputer age.

For decades, education had been only a state and not a federal issue. While voters ranked education as the most important state issue, schools barely appeared in the rankings they gave on national issues. This changed. By 1996, education was number one on the list of the most important problems voters felt were facing the nation, not just the state. Education had become a federal issue and the Republicans were caught off guard.

In a sense, the Democrats were doing with education what Nixon had done with crime—making a local issue into a national one. Capitalizing on liberal Supreme Court decisions, Nixon ran on a "law and order" platform in 1968 and again in 1972. Democrats derided Nixon's obsession with the issue as a form of racism. They lost twenty years of elections, in part because they would not take crime seriously as a federal issue.

Now the Republican efforts to slash federal education funding, as part of their Contract with America, had opened the door for Clinton to make national education programs a key federal issue. Confronting Republican demands that he abolish the Department of Education, slash Title I funding, cancel plans to expand Head Start, and end grants to promote remedial programs and counseling, Clinton railed against GOP attempts to cut "Medicare, education, Medicaid and the environment"— ME-ME. Suddenly the Republican congressional leadership came to be seen as anti-school.

Efforts by Republicans to counter the president's offensive by advocating a voucher system just fueled parental paranoia that they were against public education. Vouchers, by themselves, were popular. But in the absence of any serious plan to reform public schools, most parents saw the program as an effort to divert money from their children and spend it on somebody else's.

As Clinton's lead on the education issue grew, more women were voting for the president. Clinton continued to hammer at the education issue so dear to their hearts. While Republicans complained that their loss of womens' support was due to their pro-life position, they failed to see that their opposition to federal help for schools was also instrumental in driving away female voters.

. . .

By the time of the 1996 election, Clinton had the X Generation in his pocket. His assiduous courtship assured that he carried the under-thirty vote by nineteen points—ten points more than he had in 1992—his biggest gain among any age group.

The Xers were thrilled that a president was paying attention to their needs. Growing up in the shadow of their Boomer parents, they had become accustomed to being ignored. As Strauss and Howe put it:

> An awakening era that seemed euphoric to young adults was, to [the Xers], a nightmare of self-immersed parents, disintegrating homes, schools with conflicting missions, confused leaders . . . new public health dangers, and a 'Me Decade' economy that tipped toward the organized old and away from the voiceless young.

Clinton listened to the "voiceless young" and therein lay his appeal to them. These parents in their twenties and thirties stood by Clinton even as he obviously lived a life of which they disapproved. As the Lewinsky scandal unfolded, all the values that the X Generation had rejected in their Boomer parents seemed to be embodied in our adolescent president.

But Clinton was offering the X Generation something they wanted while the GOP was not. As the 1998 elections approached, Clinton focused on the need to hire more teachers, renovate more schools, and build more classrooms, while the Republicans worried about Monica.

Clinton also realized how important the Social Security issue was to the X Generation. Schooled to be pessimistic by the economic difficulties of their early years, the Xers worried that they would have to bear the burden of supporting their parents when Mom and Dad retired. Clinton zeroed in on Social Security and education as the '98 congressional elections came and scored gains in Congress, rather than the off-year loss of seats that history had led many to anticipate.

While news commentators and pundits, usually Boomers themselves, said that Clinton was buoyed by a good economy, the Xers stood by him more because of his social issues than his economic accomplishments. In a national survey conducted in May of 1999, 750 voters were read two statements:

A. While I think what Clinton did was wrong, I approve of the way he is handling issues like *education, health care, crime,* and a lot of other things that matter more to me than this scandal, so I'm glad he wasn't removed;

B. While I think what Clinton did was wrong, I approve of the way he is handling the *economy,* which matters more to me than this scandal, so I'm glad he wasn't removed.

The results showed that for voters over thirty-five the economy was the key, but for the under-thirty-five Generation Xers it was Clinton's success in dealing with social issues that counted more than his ability to help the economy.

COMPARISON OF MOTIVATION FOR SUPPORT OF CLINTON, BY AGE

Age Group	Motivation for Supporting Clinton	
	Social Issues	The Economy
UNDER 35	73%	54%
36–55	56	68
56–65	53	57
OVER 65	44	47

(PERCENTAGES TOTAL MORE THAN 100 SINCE VOTERS COULD CITE BOTH ECONOMIC AND SOCIAL ISSUES IF THEY WISHED.)

As the evidence of Clinton's indiscretions and misrepresentations mounted, conservatives looked to the X Generation for political support in their drive to oust Clinton. Instead, the Xers complained at the diversion of national focus to the scandal and the distraction it had caused.

To the Boomer generation, this diversion of national energies was not a big problem. What else was there to do? The economy was doing fine, energy supplies were plentiful, there was no major foreign threat, even terrorism seemed to have quieted down for the moment. But for the Xers, there were huge issues—the ones they encountered in their day-to-day attempts to raise their children, the issues Clinton had brought into focus with his "small bore" agenda. They were not so much offended by Clinton's conduct as by the refusal of the Republicans to pay attention to their needs as they wasted the nation's time with their ridiculous attempt at impeachment.

To the X Generation, impeachment was much more than just a national waste of time and energy. It was a very real threat to their families. What they most wanted to do—raise their children with a proper sense of decency and values—was being jeopardized by the impeachment process itself. Terms like oral sex became common on the nightly TV news. Parents had to confront questions about presidential kneepads. Long accustomed to prohibiting their children from watching adult shows on television, parents now had to be careful of the morning newspaper or the early evening news shows.

Because of this basic commitment to Clinton's programs, the X Generation voters criticized the Republicans for airing Clinton's behavior in public. To them it was the GOP, not the president, who was endangering the moral climate by raising in the media issues that were rarely discussed in the past, even in private. It was the Republican documents and the GOP speeches that the X Generation parents, pragmatists as always, had to keep from their children. The longer the national debate focused on sex and impeachment, the more the X Generation held it against the GOP. It mattered less what Clinton did than what the Republicans said.

There was an even more fundamental reason for the refusal of the X Generation to take up the cause of morality when the GOP blew its bugle. While these young parents did embrace the anti-drug, anti-promiscuity, anti-alcohol conservative lifestyle advocated by the Republican right, they did so for very different reasons. The parents of the Boomers, in their late fifties, sixties, or seventies, backed this stringent morality for religious or ethical reasons. Promiscuity or drug use was bad because it violated the norms of society. They flaunted hedonism and narcissism in the face of the time-honored virtues. This permissive conduct broke the rules and that is why they opposed it—in the young or in their president.

The X Generation accepted these strictures out of a pragmatic analysis of their generation's actual experience. They avoided drugs because they had seen what drugs did to their friends and older brothers. The fear of AIDS, more than the dread of perdition, led them to turn away from promiscuous sex. The huge toll in deaths of those who drove while intoxicated persuaded them to moderate their alcohol consumption. Their own experiences of coming from broken homes militated against divorce.

To many members of the X Generation, the fact that Bill Clinton continued with his predatory promiscuity was *his* problem. They saw not a moral issue in his conduct, but instead noticed that their president hadn't learned the same sad lessons they had learned. It was not a question of "how could he?" but more "why would he take that kind of a chance?" Clinton's behavior was forgivable. It was like watching someone smoke who apparently doesn't realize the harm he is doing to his own body. It's wrong, but it's his problem not yours.

The May 1999 national survey confirms that Generation Xers have a pragmatic rather than an authoritarian or religious reason for their moral behavior. In the survey, a national sample of 750 voters was read two statements about morality:

A. I believe in a strict code of morality and right and wrong which comes from God's word and the Bible. I try to live by it. Drugs and illicit sex are wrong so I don't engage in them. To do so would violate my personal moral and religious beliefs.

B. My conduct is governed more by common sense and practicality than by an abstract morality. It is more factors like the danger of AIDS, the possibility of pregnancy, and the importance of a good marriage than morality or religion that stop me from illicit sex. The bad experiences people have had with drugs and the way I have seen it mess up lives is the reason I abstain from them, not some moral judgment that drugs are wrong.

The X Generation was the only age group to identify more closely with the sentiments in the second statement.

ATTITUDES TOWARD MORALS AND SEX, BY AGE

Age Group	Which Statement Comes Closest to Your View	
	Statement A	Statement B
UNDER 35	40%	45%
36–55	52	38
56–65	54	37
OVER 65	54	32

And so the X Generation refused to join the Republicans as they manned the barricades of impeachment. The traditional Republican coalition of older and younger social conservatives was shattered as Clinton took away the Xers.

Strauss and Howe posit the theory that every other generation is activist and that they tend to overshadow their children. They point out, for example, that the Silent Generation of the '50s has lived in the shadow of their more activist GI Generation parents. Strauss and Howe note that the Silent Generation has never and likely will never elect a president. The GI Generation elected its first chief executive in 1960 when John Kennedy, of PT-109 fame, entered the White

House and elected its last when George Bush Sr., who had parachuted to safety in the Pacific, took office. Then Boomer Bill Clinton was elected, skipping entirely over the Silent Generation. The Silent Generation's only candidates—Walter Mondale and Mike Dukakis—never made it to 1600 Pennsylvania Avenue.

Strauss and Howe predict a similarly gloomy political future for the X Generation. But during the unimpeachment they held the balance of power. When the Xers sided with the president, the Republicans could no longer muster a majority for their social conservatism.

Bill Clinton had stolen the X Generation from Ronald Reagan.

.　.　.

As the X Generation assumes more political power, the role of the Internet in our politics is bound to increase. Issues like education, the environment, day care, and other parenting concerns will be catapulted to the top of our national agenda. Less focused on economic issues and more involved in values questions, these new young parents will likely have a distinctly healthy influence on American politics.

Just as the X Generation provided a needed ballast during the unimpeachment by keeping their focus on the greater national issues at stake in removing a duly elected chief executive, so their impact on politics is likely to be profound.

Young parents need a government a lot more than do older voters. Theirs are the children who use the schools, need the most police protection, are at greatest risk from drugs, use recreational facilities the most, and need jobs when they enter the workforce. It is among them that abstract moral issues meet reality. As young parents go, so eventually will the nation.

But it is these very voters who have opted out of the political world in larger numbers than any other age group. Through the Internet, politics is coming to them. By invading their computers and showing up in their e-mail, the public sphere is getting to them—literally—where they live.

As their political participation increases, the nation will be less focused on faraway or abstract issues than it will be on the here and now. It is the seriousness of these new young voters that has already moved education to the top of the national agenda after many years off it. They do not accept the theoretical point that schools should be a state and local concern. It is their children, and if it takes Washington to increase school funding and demand higher educational standards, that's fine.

Similarly, they see environmental issues as more important than does any other age group.

Their impatience with the opposition of the right wing to abortion on the one hand and gun control on the other has driven them away from the Republican Party and toward the Democrats.

The currently under-thirty-five-year-old voters, as they age, will constitute a larger and larger share of the electorate. Encouraged to participate through the Internet, they will change fundamentally our national agenda.

Chapter Six

HOW THE INTERNET WILL
CHANGE THE MEDIA

HOW MANY TIMES in recent years have we heard sociolo-
gists, journalists, and other commentators bemoan the lack of
in-depth coverage of news in our society? We hear that the thirty-
second advertisement has reduced political dialogue to the level
of demagoguery and sloganeering. The endless, wordy, philo-
sophic examination of a subject seems about to become a dead
art form.

In broadcast and print media, the financial imperative is on
ratings. Implicitly, this means reach and frequency. The pursuit
of yet another new reader or viewer becomes an obsession and
makes appeal to the more sophisticated and in-depth consumer a luxury they cannot afford. The program or the station
wants a lot of people to watch and to come back every day or
every week. The producer couldn't care less how much they
absorb. He just wants a large number of warm bodies on couches

watching his program every time it is on. The publisher doesn't much care if his subscribers use the pages of his paper to wrap fish, he just wants them to come back tomorrow and buy his paper again.

Things are about to change. The Internet will be the first medium in communications history that will care more about how absorbed a user becomes than how many users there are. On the Net it is depth (the amount of material people explore on a Web site), more than reach (the number of people contacted) or even frequency (the number of times they come back), that is the key to making money.

We have seen that the Internet is a good deal for advertisers, that a political candidate's Web banner could be seen by a million voters for a cost of only $10,000 to the campaign. So how does the owner of a site make money?

Each banner ad on a Web page can promote a product, another Web site, or just about anything. The advertiser pays the owner of the Web site anywhere from $5 to $30 for each thousand people who click onto the page containing his ad.

Each time someone visits a Web site and looks at one page— usually the home page (the first page)—an "impression" has been recorded. To calculate the total number of impressions a site garners in a month, the number of visitors is multiplied by the number of times each visitor returns by the number of pages he looks at while he is there. The following chart compares the impressions of a number of widely used Internet sites during 1998:

MONTHLY USE OF INTERNET SITES IN 1998

Site	Visitors		Visits		Impressions per Visit		Total Impressions
MSNBC	6,400	X	3.2	X	12.2	=	249,856
USA TODAY	3,900	X	3.5	X	17.8	=	242,970
CNN	7,000	X	2.8	X	11.5	=	225,400
NEW YORK TIMES	1,600	X	4.3	X	28.0	=	192,640
WASHINGTON POST	2,100	X	3.4	X	14.1	=	100,674
ABC	3,900	X	2.2	X	9.7	=	83,226
BOSTON GLOBE	2,800	X	2.0	X	13.2	=	73,920
CBS	3,100	X	2.1	X	7.0	=	45,570

The sites that get the most total impressions have the most inventory to sell to advertisers and, likely, make the most money. (There is considerable variation in these prices and because of the numerous possibilities for trade-offs, exact figures are hard to come by.) While the *New York Times,* for example, got only 1.6 million visitors in this month and CBS got twice as many, the *Times* got each visitor to come back 4.3 times while CBS got only 2.1 repeat visits. More important, the average visitor to the *New York Times* site looked at twenty-eight pages per visit while the people who logged on to CBS looked at only seven pages. The *Times* got 193 million total impressions in this sample month due to the large number of pages that each person looked at once they logged on. CBS only got 46 million—less than a quarter as many—even though it had almost twice the number of visitors.

The economics are daunting. Because of the large number of impressions, the *Times* can get four times as much money as CBS from Internet advertising on its Web site. Thus the more interesting a Web site is, the more depth and detail it provides, the more deeply it sucks in each visitor, the more page impressions it will get, the more ads it will sell, the more money it will make.

The financial imperative to get people to not only visit a site and return frequently, but also to probe its contents deeply while there, creates a revolutionary imperative for journalism. To make the reader want to stay on a site and get them to look at a large number of its pages requires the site to generate a lot of interesting material. An awful lot. The future is bright for anyone who can write and has something interesting to say. The premium is on providing extensive, interesting, engaging material to encourage visitors to click on a large number of pages and also on offering content that changes constantly to attract repeat visits.

The Internet's voracious and unquenchable appetite for material will consume ideas, facts, opinions, and comments like a whale eats plankton—in ever more massive amounts. Just as the spread of VCRs and the proliferation of cable stations together created an avaricious demand for films and videos of all descriptions, so the Internet in general, and Internet politics in particular, will generate a massive market for information.

A clue about the future comes from the recent growth of cable news channels. At present there are at least a dozen of them. With the Internet, it will be impossible to monitor what people are watching. When CNN was joined by the Fox News Channel, Court TV, C-SPAN, CNBC, and MSNBC, there developed a new kind of oracle—the expert/commentator—who will be in great demand on the Net. His or her precursor was of course the op-ed contributor to the local newspaper. On these pages the outside expert began to find a national audience by commenting, in seven hundred words per appearance, on the topic du jour.

The challenge of filling an entire day with interesting material triggered a quantum growth in the pundit business. By overwhelming traditional newsgathering techniques, cable TV stations gave the expert/commentator a vast new opportunity to be heard. Anchors talking to reporters on location in faraway parts of the globe could fill only a certain number of minutes and hours of the unforgivingly long day. So cable stations pressed into service opinion-makers, citizen-soldiers, to offer their perspectives on the news.

The O. J. Simpson trial turned into a media cash cow. Anyone who was ever remotely connected with the criminal justice system seemed to occupy the media spotlight. The entire country seemed to go to law school as it followed the trial. Legions of former and current prosecutors, judges, jurors, defense attorneys, criminologists, psychologists, forensic specialists, medical examiners, fingerprint experts, and the like were dragged before the cameras to dissect every moment of the trial of America's fallen hero.

The unimpeachment of Bill Clinton became the political sequel to the O. J. trial as a new group of experts was rounded up, made-up, and put oncamera to comment on the proceedings as they unfolded. By now the news business was huge. When the Kosovo War came, every former military officer or current strategic or weapons expert in reach found himself in front of the camera being asked every manner of question about Apache helicopters, air defense systems, and the effectiveness of air strikes.

As expertise finds more and more outlets and has to be packaged in ever more attractive ways to assure "clickership" on a Web site, the public's information levels will soar. Already driven up by cable news stations and C-SPAN, the amount Americans know about what is happening around them will rise to previously unimagined heights.

Just as we now know all the rules of evidence, thanks to the Simpson trial; the details of every weapons system, courtesy of the Kosovo and Gulf Wars; and the intricate details of Senate procedure as a result of the unimpeachment, we will find each area of political life illuminated by interesting, informative, and, above all, in-depth commentary.

Within the media a shift will come in which more power will flow to individual writers and journalists while their editors and publishers will exercise less control. Pluralism is the ally of the working press, but it is the enemy of their bosses. The Internet will do for journalism what free agency has done for baseball players. Deprived of their monopolies, media moguls will have less political power and they will have to compete for journalistic talent to fill the vast and constantly changing pages of their Web sites.

The ubiquity of the media on the Internet will destroy all the geographic and other boundaries that now fence in a journalist's stories. A reporter for the *Cleveland Plain Dealer* or a local cable station will have the same opportunity to break a big story as one whose byline appears in the nation's most prestigious news organs. With intensive research and diligent reporting, each will have a good shot at hitting the big time. The Fifth Estate will present wonderful opportunities for the working press.

But that which will make it an appealing time to be a journalist will also diminish the political power of the owners and publishers of the press as their monopolies erode. If New Yorkers can read the *Los Angeles Times* as easily as the *Baltimore Sun,* the power of the hometown paper diminishes.

Though the power of the owners and publishers of the nation's newspapers and television networks is about to drop precipitously, their financial rewards will likely rise as quickly as their political clout declines. The infinite demand for material that the Internet will create will undoubtedly make the business of hiring writers and turning out electronic and printed material more remunerative than ever.

The impact of the Internet on the press will be like the change VCRs brought to the entertainment industry. With the vast reach of videocassette recorders, the demand for new video material swelled proportionately. While in-theater movie revenues have only grown from $24 per person per year in 1990 to a projected $27 in 2001, home-video spending has soared from $56 per person in 1990 to $96 in 1999, with a projected $114 by 2001.

For writers the most noticeable change in the complexion of the media under the Fifth Estate is that the substance of the story will become far more important than where it is placed. If one million people read the *New York Times* and four hundred thousand read the *New York Post,* an article in the *Times* will obviously reach more people than will one in the *Post.*

When the Internet becomes omnipresent, this simple equation will no longer be true. Tens of millions of people will have the opportunity to access both the story in the *Times* and the one in the *Post.* The question will be how many people will click on to each article to read it. It will be the interest the story generates, not the respect its organ commands, that determines how widely it is read or how influential it becomes. Of course one newspaper's Web site might attract more users than another's, but eventually users will find their way to any site to read a story that strikes their interest. The brand name will count for little. The content will become the only important variable.

This increasing democratization of access to readers will make the lesser organs of journalism more important. No longer will a handful of top reporters control most headline stories. Obviously, some journalists will continue to be better than others. Nothing will ever reduce the clout of top reporters like Bob Woodward of the *Washington Post* or Jeff Gerth of the *New York Times.* But now reporters in Peoria will be able to compete in the big time as their articles leapfrog their normal print circulation and go out over the Net.

The underlying premises of journalism will change in the Internet era. Today each newspaper or television station tries to be the place where their readers or viewers first learn what is happening in the world. Each paper or station covers virtually the same stories on the front page or in the first ten minutes of the newscast. Only local stories differ. They compete for special angles, try to be first with the scoop, and vie for analytical depth, but their coverage is more similar than it is different. This causes a follow-the-pack mentality, which journalistic observers like James Fallows have decried, wherein a few reporters tell the rest of the journalistic Establishment what to think.

While today a reader or viewer tends to watch only one TV news show and pick up only one newspaper, in the future he will browse the Net reading or watching whatever interests him. This creates a premium on diversity, not on duplication. The new story, the scoop, becomes far more important than just parroting the coverage offered in all other organs. Indeed, it's a lot better to produce a new slant on the tenth most important thing that happened that day than to pile on with the tenth account of the one most important story.

This emphasis on variety rather than redundancy will contribute to the fattening of the wallets and the power of the average reporter. The range of items that will make it into the news stream will expand dramatically as everyone seeks to attract new readers with new, not duplicative, material.

Even the prioritization that now dominates print and television news will change. Currently you either are on the front page or you're not. Your story either makes the top of the newscast or it is buried. The physical ordering of the newspaper, with only one front page, and the sequencing of televised news are unforgiving. But on the Internet it matters a lot less *where* the story is listed. The home page of a Web site can list all stories of note, not just a few. Most likely, viewers will click on areas of interest. Rather than notice only the three or four political stories that make it to page one or are covered in the half-hour TV news program, Web visitors can click on "politics" and instantly access ten or twenty stories that in a newspaper would be consigned to die a slow death on page C23. In television they would litter the editing-room floor. But the Web site is an equal-opportunity news outlet.

Chapter Seven

CAMPAIGNING TO WIN
THE FIFTH ESTATE

AS THE INTERNET replaces television as the locus for political campaigns, the nature and content of political speech will change completely. Political campaigns of the future will differ totally from those being waged today. The difference will be as great as the gap between pre-television campaigning and modern ad-based candidacies. The change in the medium will force a change in the message.

The basic premises of today's political communication are brevity, focus, repetition, and condensation. In the Internet era, elaboration, explanation, and extrapolation will be the primary virtues.

Just as the stars of silent movies found it hard to weather the transition to talkies, and radio actors found adjustment to television difficult, so the kind of politicians, advertising experts, media creators, political consultants, and leaders who have thrived in the era of television will find it hard to meet the new challenges of Internet campaigning. Some will make the switch, others will fail.

The first step in a successful transition is to recognize the fundamental differences between television and Internet campaigning and to recognize the new imperatives the Net will impose on those who seek to be elected.

THE VOLUNTARY CAMPAIGN

Today, paid political advertising is based on the premise of involuntary communication. Nobody chooses to watch political ads. When we are sitting on the couch looking at our favorite shows on the tube, an ad comes on and we find ourselves forced to watch. We could get up, but the couch is so very comfortable. Turn the TV off? What? And miss the start of the next segment? We're trapped. We've got to watch.

Over the Internet, there are no traps. We can go to whichever Web sites we want. Even if a campaign pays for an advertisement to be displayed as a banner at the top of another Web site, we hold in our hand the decision to click or not to click, to view or not to view. The exposure to political information over the Internet is entirely and completely voluntary.

This difference between choice and coercion is crucial. The voluntarism will force an entirely different kind of campaigning on our system. Currently, those who run campaigns work hard to determine what programs voters watch so that they can lie in wait with their political messages and pounce on the unwary voter during commercial interruptions. Those who design commercials do their best to draw the voter in before he or she realizes that it is a political ad. How many times have we seen a moving human drama unfold in an ad only to discover that it's actually a political commercial? The entire emphasis in political campaigning today is to entrap the voter.

In Internet campaigning, no force-feeding is possible. At the very worst, a candidate can run a message on the screen that won't disappear until the user clicks on the tiny box that says "no thanks." In the first few weeks of Internet use, we all become expert at finding that box without reading or even really noticing the ad. All we feel is resentment for having to make that extra click in order to do what we want to when we log on.

The aim of Internet campaigning will be to run so attractive a message that voters will want to watch. The entire equation will be different. The stress will be on that attraction, not on catching the voter unawares. A voter must want to get campaign information to find it on the Net.

An entire generation of campaign advertising based on involuntary learning will go out of style. The Pavlovian idea of repetition that conditions an essentially memorized and automatic response will go out the window. Ads that are designed to make us remember the name and attributes of a candidate by repeating their themes over and over will not do the trick. Voters will just choose not to click.

.   .   .

In this sense, Internet campaigning has more in common with traditional journalism than it does with political propaganda. The newspaper or TV station must provide a sufficiently attractive program for the viewer to choose to watch it. Just as the headline must grab the reader's attention and enlist his interest, so the banner advertising a candidate's Web site must be alluring and stimulating. Political information will have to be packaged attractively and presented appealingly. For the first time in modern political history, there will be a premium on getting the voter's interest rather than merely on catching him while he's doing something else. Internet political campaigning has to make the voter desire the information and want to be moved. Political campaigning that does not interest the voter won't get through.

Candidates will have to focus on issues, ideas, and substance to persuade the electorate to click on their sites. Negative commercials will be much more difficult since they are unlikely to interest anyone. Humor will play an increasing role.

Political information will not only have to be packaged attractively and presented appealingly, but it will also have to engage the voter with humor and innovation. The prototype may be the new genre of ads running on cable stations directed to online investors. Whether one is interested in such a venture or not, we all smile at the creative and truly funny ads about tow truck drivers who have come to own islands through their investing savvy and airheads who think that "the market" is the grocery store.

This new emphasis on actually *attracting* voters rather than just imposing one's message upon them will help stimulate political interest and voter turnout. Right now, campaigns just have to persuade voters, they don't have to entice them. We know that the habitual voter will be in the voting booth on election day. All we have to do these days is to get him to vote one way or the other.

DRAWING THE VOTER IN

Repetition won't work on the Internet.

Today political campaigns are based on the idea of repetition, constantly seeking to hit voters over and over again with the same basic idea until they involuntarily learn it.

"Stay on message," consultants are forever advising candidates, lest they wander and think creatively as they campaign for public office. Keeping a candidate "on message" is vital to our current political campaigns, so that there is enough repetition of the same message for it to sink in.

But in Internet campaigning the rules will be totally different. Internet users will be bored out of their minds by the same thirty-second canned message every time they click on a site. In order to remain attracted to a candidate, these voters will demand and expect new material, interesting insights, and poignant messages each time they click on, or soon another candidate's Web site will spring up and engage their attention.

To keep a voter interested, involved, and, therefore, committed, the new rules will place a premium on depth rather than on repetition, on elaboration rather than on condensation.

All the skills of modern television political consultants are aimed at compression. Ads can run only for thirty seconds (unless one is wealthy enough to afford sixties), so the goal is to reduce the content of the entire campaign to thirty seconds. It is not an insurmountable task. One prominent political consultant once said he could think of a lot of messages that could be fully expressed in thirty seconds or even less. "I love you, I hate you, I'm going to kill you." All these ideas, he contended, could be expressed in much less than thirty seconds and would still convey great meaning. "Our politicians just don't have a lot to say," he concluded sadly.

A candidate will need to expand on his themes and ideas in order to keep his Web site supplied with material. Position papers, long consigned to the file cabinets of political campaigns, will have new relevance as Web users will want to explore the nuances and details of their candidate's position. The discipline to which campaigns will have to yield will not be that of endless conformity, but of constant creativity.

The sheer volume of material that Internet campaigning will consume will present a formidable challenge to the one-idea-at-a-time brains of most modern political operatives. Their skills in boiling down messages to their core—learned over a lifetime—will have to be reversed.

The best way for a campaign to generate interest in its message is to apply it to the daily unfolding of events.

Just as the Voice of America or Radio Free Europe sought to explain the virtues of freedom in the context of each day's news, so an Internet campaign must relate its ideology and world view to the events of the moment and use them to articulate and elaborate the reasons behind their candidate's agenda. A campaign that features gun control as part of its platform will want to report developments in the school shootings of 1999 in light of its views on limiting the availability of handguns and other weapons. A candidacy that promotes more defense spending would do well to present the difficulties the military experienced in Kosovo to illustrate its case that better equipment and more readiness are important.

In television campaigning, messages are essentially strategic rather than tactical. The campaign usually films its ads well before they run and uses them to articulate the central themes of the race. Only later, nearer election day, in the give-and-take of political dialogue and debate, does the campaign tailor its message to the realities of what the opposition is saying. Attacks must be rebutted. Each campaign vies to seize the offensive. But even at this harried time at the end of a campaign, the same ad runs for a week or more. As TV viewership drops, campaigns sometimes have to leave the same message on the air for weeks to get through to the voters.

Internet campaigns will have to be much more tactical than strategic to remain current and relevant. Most of our current crop of consultants will not be up to the challenge. They will find themselves intellectually overwhelmed by the task of creating daily messages and will yearn for the days of television campaigning when one thirty-second ad could and should last for two or three weeks. They will be over their heads trying to develop the in-depth messages that the Internet necessitates.

If today's political campaigns can be said to stem from an intellectual heritage, it is that of advertising. The techniques that help sell a product are akin to those that modern advertising gurus use to promote political candidacies. By contrast, Internet campaigning will have to come from the intellectual heritage of journalism to be equal to the task of keeping tens of millions of voters interested.

The problems a reporter or an editor faces in getting someone to read a newspaper article are similar to the challenges of stimulating an Internet user to click on a Web site. In one case it is the headline that attracts, in the other it is the banner at the top of another Web site. In both instances the important thing is to interest the reader and get him to go deeper into the article.

Compelling graphics and visual creativity will be at a premium in Internet campaigning, where messages must be alluring, humorous, attractive, and entertaining. Web-site users expect as much from the sites onto which they log.

.   .   .

In today's television-dominated political campaigns, it is the programming that provides the entertainment and the attraction. The ads are merely adjacent to the programs. But in the Internet era, it will be up to the campaign itself to generate the entertainment values.

In modern TV campaigns, the political communications reflect the campaign's needs. What does the campaign need to tell the voter? What message must the candidate send to win? But in the Internet era, the voter's interests and wishes will be definitive. What message most interests and engages the Web-site visitor? How can we make his interests and our political needs intersect? These will be the dominant questions.

The effects on voter turnout are likely to be dramatic. If Internet campaigns need to reach out and present gripping messages to get voters to read them, candidates will stimulate turnout by their efforts. Each ad will be a recruitment poster for politics in general as well as a specific candidate in particular. Campaigns will have to get voters to click the "read" button, not the "delete" button. They will need to encourage people to click on the banner that comes across the top of the screen, "Bush for President" or "Hillary for the Senate." They will have to encourage and stimulate voluntary participation. If they succeed in doing so, the effect of Internet voting will be to increase the number of voters in regular elections.

It has already been demonstrated that interesting campaigns attract larger turnouts. When Ross Perot articulated an exciting new message in 1992, getting almost 20 percent of the vote, he drove voter participation up sharply. The Internet will stimulate turnout in a way we have not seen in our political system in decades. Politics will become interesting enough to get more of us to vote, finally.

TARGETING WITH LASERS

Hit and miss will be a thing of the past in the brave new world of the Internet. Like planes with smart bombs, Internet advertising agencies will be able to target a candidate's message with laserlike specificity to separate and distinct voting groups.

Targeting in today's politics is exceedingly blunt and flawed. With only a handful of programs on television to choose from at any given hour of the day, every advertiser is reaching a lot of people he doesn't want to target. An ad placed on a daytime soap opera will, of course, reach a bunch of married, stay-at-home women. But it will also hit hundreds of thousands of other consumers who aren't in the market for diapers or dishwasher detergent. As cable television has expanded the range of media outlets, targeting can become somewhat more precise. But it remains haphazard at best.

On the Internet, Web sites tend to be closely tailored to discreet subject areas. You know whom you are reaching when you put an ad on a Web site about health care for the elderly. Likewise, a banner advertisement that runs on a movie Web site is going to hit certain types of consumers. Targeting can be refined to a degree that is impossible in the current media environment. For example, Internet political advertisements in a congressional race could target those who do not believe in the government's explanation of the Waco debacle, those who favored impeachment of the president, or those who favor school vouchers. By reaching into the interests of each voter and advertising on the Web site that epitomizes them, Internet advertising can achieve its target in a way far superior to traditional media advertising. By targeting the message and the audience and matching them precisely, a candidate can use Internet advertising powerfully to attract new supporters.

A banner ad aimed at voters who protest the Justice Department's tactics in its raid on David Koresh and his followers might read "Do you think Reno is telling the truth on Waco? I don't. Click here to help get the truth out." The click would trigger an Internet voyage to the candidate's Web site, where the voter would learn all about him and his positions. Similarly, an incumbent could target the same Web site and publicize his calls for an investigation of the Waco raid. Thus a candidate introduces himself to the voters directly in their faces by showing his empathy with their specific areas of interest and commitment.

As a result, candidates can send individual messages out to each different segment of the electorate. No longer will they broadcast their messages. Instead, they will have the ability to narrowcast them. Candidates will fall all over one another to be as specific as possible in addressing the concerns of those who frequent each particular Web site. Broad general messages will tend to be lost as campaigns hone in on what each group of Internet users wants as they tap into their favorite Web sites.

In this new era, advertising will become very focused and the feedback on its effectiveness will be instantaneous. Candidates and nonpolitical advertisers as well will be able to immediately gauge which ads are working. Every day they will get a summary of how many "hits" each ad drew. If an ad fails to get the requisite number of "clicks"—people clicking on it to get the details—it isn't working and it can be changed immediately. This laserlike monitoring will lead to more economical, more efficient, and more effective advertising. Campaigns on the Internet will cost less as their efficiency rises and they get the right message to the right voters.

THE IMPORTANCE OF INTERACTIVITY

Political communication today is a one-way street. The candidate talks and the voter listens. This enforced passivity is likely one of the major reasons for the decline in voter interest and turnout. Who wants always to listen and never to speak? Who has the patience to absorb candidates' messages for months, with only a few seconds in the voting booth in which to respond? It is no wonder that the process is alienating.

On the Internet, interactivity is the norm. Internet campaigning will feature a lively give-and-take between the voter and the candidate.

In this new world, candidates will actually have to let voters talk and will have to pay attention to what they say. The campaign that affords the most engaging interactivity and gives voters the best chance to be heard will be the most successful in keeping the voters' attention. Responsiveness will be the key.

As citizens become accustomed to voting in Internet referendums on important national, state, and local issues, they will look for opportunities to influence the thinking of a campaign and a candidate rather than sit back passively and await his message. They will insist on speaking to their favorite candidates.

Talk radio and Internet chat rooms currently come the closest to approximating the new world of Internet interactivity. The call-in format used by hosts like Rush Limbaugh and Michael Reagan is a portent of things to come. Just as people adore the opportunity to be heard over the air asking questions or making comments, so the interactivity of a candidate's Web site will prove a big allure. By the hundreds of thousands, voters will want to talk on the Net to the campaigns and to the candidates they are thinking of supporting. As they now do on talk radio, they will expect to be heard. They will want the candidates to listen.

Chat rooms and discussion boards on Web sites serve not only as a vent for opinions, but also as a virtual community. Alienated and fragmented, Americans are desperately searching for communities. Moving from home to home, state to state, region to region, they lack that sense of neighborhood that is often so crucial to a proper feeling of identity and belonging.

John DeMaria, marketing director of Environments.com, puts it well: "Through chat rooms and e-mail, voters can aggregate their power and force change in the political system. In the past, for example, ten million voters might contact members of Congress on a specific issue. But their isolation adds to their powerlessness. When those voices, however, are aggregated on the Internet and expressed to their elected representatives, they gain a unique power. Rather than ten million individual peashooters that merely annoy the dragon, they become a unified missile that slays it." Or at least changes its mind.

Internet users are usually enthusiastic participants in chat rooms where they find people who share their interests, beliefs, and outlook. It is a measure of how starved we are for interaction that people will wait on the phone for an hour or more to get to ask a question or make a comment on the air or will talk with total strangers in an Internet chat room, just to be heard by someone.

The Internet allows those who are shy or retiring, or just want to remain anonymous, to express themselves without going to a meeting, giving a speech, or joining a group. The unique ability to speak out without having to talk in public, which characterizes e-mail and chat rooms, gives the less aggressive among us a chance to be heard.

Whenever America wishes to be heard, it overwhelms chat rooms and talk shows with messages and phone calls. Desperate to pour out their feelings to others in times of crisis or national tragedy, people turn to the Net when there is a massacre at Littleton or a John Kennedy Jr. is missing. This desire to reach out to others, once gratified in churches or PTA meetings, is a massive energy force into which the Internet taps.

Like talk-radio shows, the Web sites of a candidate will attract not only supporters but also curious onlookers if they offer an exciting format and stimulating discussion. Politics will have to go retail and win votes one at a time rather than attempt to wholesale them through mass media and advertising. This renewed focus on the individual will do much to reduce alienation and bring in new voters to the system.

Just as talk-radio hosts cover a wide range of interesting topics for discussion, political Web sites will compete to bring their message to bear on events as they unfold. If there is another hideous incident of school violence, for example, candidates will take to their Web sites to talk online with supporters and potential converts about the issues the shootings raise. All events of the day will become campaign issues. Candidates and officeholders will have to respond to current affairs in order to keep voters connected with their Web sites.

The basic rule is simple. Voters are going to spend a certain amount of time online every day. If your campaign does not give them an interesting and attractive place to hang out on the Net, some other campaign will. There is nothing more dangerous for a candidate than to leave his supporters home alone on the Net without compelling material to grab and keep their attention.

It will be daunting to meet the technical challenge of making a Web site interesting to all voters. Good graphics will be only the starting point. Campaigns will have to get volunteers or paid staff to talk with voters through interactive e-mail. Successful candidates will need to provide outlets through which voters can vent their opinions. Dialogues between and among supporters via chat rooms and other interactive vehicles will be essential.

Campaigns will stage Internet rallies—times of day when supporters of a candidate will gather electronically to hear virtual speeches and correspond with one another. Virtual coffee klatches—sans coffee, but allowing voters to "talk" with the candidate through the Internet interviews—will become staples of modern campaigning. Managed chats, where a moderator answers questions and provides a structured dialogue, will become more prevalent.

The commitment to interactivity has its roots in the experiences of younger as opposed to middle-aged or older voters. Those reared in the passivity of the television age are not used to talking back. Couch potatoes since infancy, they are conditioned to remain docile and wait for the programming to entertain them. But the X Generation, trained by interactive games, wants to connect with television, not just watch it. Their children, the Millennium Generation, are being reared on the computer and will demand interactivity even more.

.   .   .

As the campaign remains responsive, so of course must the candidate. In Internet political campaigning, the model of television will have to be replaced by that of talk radio, which is built around the opportunity it affords ordinary people to have an audience for their views. Campaign Web sites will not only be able to listen to what the constituents say, they will also have to help broadcast those views. Chat rooms and other interactive processes will predominate. The candidate who is in love with his own voice will have to make way for the one who interacts with people, listens to them, and lends himself to broadcasting their views as well as his own.

Just as the Senate became filled with blow-dried candidates who exuded charisma in the television age, it will now fill up with men and women who are as skilled at listening as they are at speaking. Interactive leaders, they will have mastered the art of catalyzing public opinion and helping to transform it into political action.

E-MAILING TO VICTORY

E-mail will be the new frontier for politicians. Free, immediate, and interactive, it presents an incredible opportunity to campaigns of the future. Both as a fundraising vehicle and as a way to communicate with huge numbers of voters instantly, e-mail will revolutionize politics—for good and for bad.

Imagine the scene: A candidate is falling behind as election day nears. Where once he was comfortably ahead, his adversary is gaining, first creeping up and now galloping hard on his heels. Our campaign manager hears the ominous footsteps closing in. The solution? A new TV ad? Too few people are watching on any given night to make much of a difference. Besides, it's Sunday and the election is Tuesday. The most an ad could do is to run for one night—Monday. Hardly enough to make much of a difference. A speech? The media won't give it the coverage he'd need and the press would likely butcher the message anyway.

Enter e-mail. Write a statement attacking the opponent's position on a significant issue and appeal for votes. Send it instantly to millions and millions of voters. Just a click and the comforting "your mail has been sent" message appears. But then what happens? The other side e-mails its own message in response. Incredibly, with the polls about to open, a full rebuttal and counter-attack goes out to the same voters you reached with your Sunday-night strike. Is there time for another round? Hell, yes. In the instant world of e-mail, communications never stop. Entire campaigns, with intense dialogue between the two sides, can take place in an hour.

Once campaigns took months to get a message out. With TV ads, it takes about a week to get a full hearing. With e-mail, it takes a nanosecond. The result is that campaign dialogues will become incredibly more intricate, rushed, last minute, and will continue right up to the wire! Just as nuclear weapons could reduce the length of a war to an hour, the e-mail campaign will condense months of dialogue into a few minutes. Like onlookers at a professional tennis match, the voters will turn their heads back and forth watching the play as e-mail messages whiz first one way and then the other. For campaign operatives, endgame strategies will become immensely important.

Campaigns will increasingly correspond with vast numbers of voters interactively to get support, recruit volunteers, raise money, and energize their bases. The key will be to have good e-mail lists. Companies will make huge amounts of money selling lists of vot-ers' e-addresses. No campaign will dare go without the best and most up-to-date lists.

There is currently very little regulation to prevent massive e-mailing. The Internet community spends millions of dollars a year to block unsolicited mail and has, so far, been relatively effective in its self-policing. But once politicians get into the act, this purity is unlikely to last. Just as voters coquettishly guarded their privacy in the nineteenth century but now submit to listing in phone books for all to see, it is inevitable that unsolicited e-mailings will become ubiquitous.

Will these e-mail messages be "spam"—the derisive term for unwanted and unsolicited mail? Not necessarily. Unlike most other mail, these messages will not be fundraising solicitations. They will bring information that voters will value as the campaign unfolds.

Internet e-mail campaigning will pass important facts and arguments to voters who, after all, follow the debate because they need to make up their minds. As election day approaches, the dizzying pace of e-mailing will likely energize voters and stimulate an even higher turnout. People will enjoy the prospect of reading each campaign's message and weighing their relative merit. If the process proves onerous, there is no such thing as involuntary communications on the Net. It remains only to click on "delete" and, presto, a message is gone! It will be the task of campaigns to make their messages sufficiently interesting, informative, and interactive to get voters to click on "read" instead.

A FLIGHT INTO THE FUTURE

(This section was prepared based on the inspiration of Frank Baraff, a New York political consultant blessed with equal parts imagination and creativity.)

. . .

Imagine the campaign of the future. You go home and turn on your television/telephone/computer, hooked up by broadband, and you click on Bush.com. On comes George Bush (by now it will be one of the grandsons) in living color.

You'll ask, "What is your position on global warming?" He'll answer.

"But," you'll object, "you voted against the global warming bill in Congress."

Video George will explain why he thought the bill was flawed and will point out that he voted for a substitute bill that he thought was better.

"But the Sierra Club opposed the bill you introduced," you'll remind the candidate.

"Sure they did," he'll answer, "they wanted to raise taxes to fund their bill and I felt that would be too costly."

And so forth. For all you know, this is really George Bush speaking to you in person. And it sort of is. It's just that Bush's media expert will have filmed hundreds of hours of conversations with his candidate, exploring the ramifications of every single issue or topic you are likely to raise. Then, through a series of prompts that you trigger by your comments and questions, the computer selects the appropriate Bush response and on comes the tape of him saying it.

The difference between an effective and an ineffective campaign will lie, in part, in how thoroughly the media experts anticipate the questions of the voters and how well they can work with the candidate to give the right responses.

The goal of this interactive campaign is not to fool the voter. People will, of course, realize that they are not actually speaking to George Bush. They will be well aware that they are conversing with a videotaped recording of him, but all the words the video speaks will actually be Bush's words, his content, his program, and his meaning. Because he will have spent the endless hours needed to record each element of the dialogue, it will also reflect his mannerisms and personality. It will be, literally, the best way of getting to know him short of actually spending several hours in his company.

The process will not be much different than the software now inside the candidate's brain. After lots of preparation and coaching, he's in effect "programmed" to give the right responses to the comments or questions of the press or the public. All that will be different is that the electric connects that now go on inside the candidate's mind will occur inside the campaign computer instead. The job of the media expert will be to replicate the circuitry so accurately that he can bring the same spontaneity and style to the virtual conversation that the candidate would impart to a real one.

The necessity of anticipating the questions the voter will ask and of responding, in advance, to each one will force campaigns to flesh out their ideas with far more depth and precision than they do today. Reporters will log on to conduct virtual conversations with the candidate and will report on controversial elements in his platform. The video library behind these virtual conversations will be a kind of oral history—told in contemporary times—of his campaign.

When last-minute developments take place in a campaign, or an opponent runs a negative ad attacking Bush, on he will come at the click of a button on your home computer with an interactive message rebutting the charges. Once again it will feel and sound like a conversation with Bush, but it will be virtual, not real. Today when a candidate throws or receives a negative attack, the voter is left to choose between two thirty-second versions of the truth. Sometimes there is an impartial referee in the form of the media to umpire the conflict, but much of the time the media, too, is left guessing about the facts. When campaigns are waged through virtual conversations between candidates and voters, the voters will be able to probe and ask detailed questions in order to get at the truth.

This communication will permit a depth and interactivity that will boggle the minds of those accustomed to the he-talks-and-we-listen campaigns of today. When voters suggest ideas that are outside the candidate's data bank of responses, the wise campaign will listen, absorb the message, and tailor a response. They may even be smart enough to adopt the suggestion and make it their own.

These virtual conversations will be key elements in future campaigns. There will be no one message. In politics, one size will no longer fit all. Voters will not have to eavesdrop on interviews between the press and the candidate. They will be the interviewer, getting personalized and tailored responses to each inquiry, not unlike what the reporter gets in today's televised interview.

In rudimentary form, all the technologies we need for this kind of futuristic campaign actually exist today. Already computers are being developed that respond to speech, not the written word. Speech- and voice-recognition technology is available on many 800-number phone lines where the voice of the respondent is interpreted and processed. The artificial intelligence necessary for this capability will expand in the next few years to permit the level of interactivity that a virtual conversation would require.

Broadband wiring, the type used in most cable-TV systems— which would be required to carry so extensive a load of data— is already installed in over sixty million American homes. Many Web sites offer "streaming video," the name given to the not-yet-perfected picture quality of films or movies over the Internet. In the future, computers will focus far more on video than on text. As the computer and the television merge, the text-based computers of today will seem like the telegraph compared with the telephone.

Search engines now answer questions that are asked in plain English; they need not be asked using computer jargon. Just as these technologies are calibrated to respond to verbal prompts, the computer in the virtual conversation is able to trigger the appropriate candidate response based on what the voter has asked or said.

The candidate isn't the only one that the campaigns might select for participation in virtual conversations. Perhaps the candidate's spouse or prominent political supporters might join in the fun. Men and women from out of the candidate's past might tell stories or anecdotes to give us insights into his or her personality and character. Issues experts who work for the candidate might be available for a virtual discussion in their particular area of knowledge.

Eventually it is even possible that presidential addresses will be given virtually over the Internet. One can imagine a president speaking interactively with us in our homes as he launches a legislative initiative. The virtual interactivity will make presidential addresses much more like town meetings, a specialty of President Clinton's.

The increasing capacity for one-on-one dialogue between candidates and voters will do a great deal to bridge their estrangement from one another. When a candidate can come into one's own home for a personal chat over the computer, the effect will be electrifying, just as it was when we first heard a president's voice over radio in FDR's fireside chats.

Chapter Eight

THE END OF POLLING

THE ANESTHETIZATION of our political process starts with polling. Politicians hire pollsters to tell them what people think. The polls are secret and private and even those polled don't know for whom the survey was conducted or what the results of it were. Neither the interviewers nor the participants have the faintest idea of the real purpose of the survey. It is totally sterile and antiseptic.

Just as the hospital nurse checks her patient's blood pressure and temperature every few hours, meticulously and silently recording her findings on the chart that is kept at the nurses' station well out of the patient's reach or view, so political polling excludes even those few who are selected to participate from having easy access to the results. The questions are asked at the behest of the candidate for whom the survey is taken.

The answers are neatly arranged in multiple-choice format by the survey research professional so as to create order in cataloguing the potentially chaotic and disorderly feelings of those they question. Passion is not recorded. Nor are gestures, tone of voice, general demeanor. The mother who anxiously bemoans the way her child's future is wasting away in bad schools with inept teachers becomes just a click on a computer program signifying her interest in education. The process is profoundly alienating and bloodless.

Superficial resemblances aside, Internet voting has little in common with political polling. Instead of asking only a handful of respondents, millions are involved. People can initiate the dialogue themselves by sponsoring referendums over the Internet. The results are not secret in any sense, but will be broadcast instantly and massively over the Net. In polling, the politician is the active player and the voters are passive. In Internet voting it is the people who are the activists and the initiators, and the politicians who must wait their turn and listen to what the people say.

The Internet is already encroaching on the turf of traditional political-polling techniques. A novel Web site launched by pollsters Lou Harris and Gordon Black is conducting polling over the Internet for the 2000 election. Rather than phone thousands of people to get a few hundred to participate in their surveys, they are prequalifying tens of thousands of Internet users and listing their demographic information in their database. When they need to find one hundred White Catholics for a survey in

New York State, they just consult their computer and pull out the relevant e-mail addresses. Then they invite those people to participate in the survey over the Internet.

Harris and Black's efforts have come under fire from conventional polling organizations who maintain that Internet users are disproportionately White, male, and well educated. They express the concern that even within certain set demographic parameters, the Internet polling is skimming off the cream of the electorate and failing to capture the opinions of the average voter.

Internet polling is very different from Internet voting. The former attempts to ask a statistically valid sample of Americans a question to get their views. The latter asks anyone who is interested enough in the issue to log on, of their own initiative, to be heard. Internet voting is more like writing your congressman, in the electronic age, than it is akin to the process of survey research. But, in many ways, it is a lot more valid.

For one thing, the number of people who participate in an Internet referendum will undoubtedly dwarf the number who are surveyed, whether the interviews are in person, by phone, or over the Net. When a million people vote on the Net, the information it yields about demographic groups is far more reliable than could ever be possible when only a thousand or so people are polled.

In a sample of one thousand likely voters nationally (typical sample size in today's polling) only about one hundred will be Black. Only sixty will be Hispanic. Only thirty will be Hispanic women. Only ten will be single Hispanic women. Soon the size of each subset of the electorate becomes *de minimis* and affords no accurate indicator of anything. In Internet voting, the hundreds of thousands or millions of participants will make analysis much more reliable and accurate.

Some will object that the millions who will participate in Internet voting are not representative of the general population. Academically, this is true. But polling itself has moved away from being statistically representative of the general population. Political polls that survey everybody are derided as worthless since they make no distinction between those who are registered to vote and those who are not. Even polls of voters are usually dismissed since they do not separate those who are likely to vote from voters who habitually stay home. Increasingly, pollsters don't really bother to measure what everybody thinks. Rather, they want to know what registered voters who are very likely to vote think. It is only their opinions that matter to their clients.

Where the polling relates to issues as opposed to voting intentions, pollsters are increasingly even more selective, focusing mainly on those who feel deeply about the issue and paying less heed to those whose views are more casual. Where once survey researchers asked only if voters "support or oppose" a proposal like capital punishment, now they ask if respondents "strongly support, somewhat support, somewhat oppose, or strongly oppose" the death penalty. In briefing their clients, they place particular emphasis on those polled who hold their opinions strongly, mentally screening out the views of those who don't really care about the issue in question.

Internet voting is really just an extension of these screening methods. It measures intensity in a way that survey research never really can. Just as pollsters don't ask nonvoters what they think, so the Internet voting process will sort out those who don't feel strongly enough about the issue to make time to participate. The opinions of people who take the initiative to log on and vote in an Internet referendum are precisely the ones who are likely to remember the issue when they vote in the actual election. Those who do not are likely to forget all about the issue by election day.

The essential weakness of survey research is that the pollster may not ask the right questions. The poet Robert Frost once said that "poetry is about the grief and politics is about the grievance." Too often polltakers do not grasp the grief and they fail to articulate the grievance. Since a poll is only as good as its questions, any survey that doesn't ask about the issues that really motivate people will miss the point entirely.

In his State of the Union speech of 1996, for example, President Clinton addressed a range of issues that did not appear on the traditional political radar screens. He focused on topics like violence on television, teen smoking, national educational standards, school construction, and other areas that had never been part of the traditional congressional agenda. As he won the allegiance of an entire generation of parents of young children, it became clear that these issues had indeed been of paramount importance to tens of millions of voters, but the politicians never noticed because their pollsters never asked the right questions. In Internet voting, the voters will both ask and answer the questions themselves.

Every year, it seems, issues emerge from the bowels of America and come to dominate the political dialogue. In the '70s it was abortion and the Equal Rights Amendment. In the early '80s it was the demand for tax cuts at the state and federal level and the demand for less use of nuclear power by utilities. As the decade progressed, attention turned to term limits for elected officials and tougher anticrime sentencing laws. In the '90s, curbs on affirmative action, restrictions on gun ownership, limitations on social benefits for illegal immigrants, restrictions on smoking, and a host of other issues came to dominate our politics.

Where did these issues come from? To the politicians, it seemed that they came from "nowhere." But issues that seem to spring forth spontaneously emerge from the deeply held concerns and worries of large groups of the voters. The reason they seem to take our political process by surprise and by storm is that nobody ever asks the voters what *they* think. Pollsters love to ask questions with yes-no or support-oppose answers. But these questions really test the pollsters' opinions, not the voters'. Since it is the survey researcher who writes the questions, the voters are confined to the passive role of answering them. Only rarely do pollsters ask voters to describe, in their own words, what they want and how they feel. By contrast, the very essence of the Internet is interactivity.

Once Internet voting and polling become the norm, new issues will arise out of the practical, real-life experiences of people. Politicians do not lead real lives. They read about them in the newspaper and they watch what they think is real life on television, but even if they were reared in poverty during their youth, the memories are distant and obscure to most successful politicians. The greatest struggle for a caring and concerned political leader is to remain in touch with the needs of the average person, needs he himself has left far behind. As Rudyard Kipling put it, you need to be able to "walk with kings nor lose the common touch." With the Internet, it will be easy. Real people will have a place at the table, able to articulate their ideas and propose solutions grounded in their day-to-day experiences with actual problems.

As voters feel able to impact the political process, their alienation will decrease. The cultural divide that separates those who participate from those who don't will be bridged by the interactivity of the Net. The demographics of the electorate will change completely.

Periodically our political process is invaded by these new "barbarians at the gates," the habitual nonvoters. They can be heard every day on talk-radio shows, venting their opinions well into the night. They rallied to the candidacy of Ross Perot in 1992. Of the 18 percent of the vote that the Independent candidate won, about half was cast by people who likely would not have voted had the maverick not been running. They were also much in evidence in the successful bid of former professional wrestler Jesse "The Body" Ventura to become the governor of Minnesota on the Reform Party ticket in a three-way election in 1998.

Political ferment over the Internet will replace the enforced passivity of a politics that measures public opinion by polling. The Internet will help bring the nonparticipants back into the game by eliminating the distinction between spectators and players that keeps them bored in the stands while others take the field and have the fun. Restless with the confining role of observers, they chafe and look for ways to become active. The political process is devoted to locking them out and letting in only those genteel enough to know their place. The Internet will change this equation and give them a way to participate, even at 2:00 A.M. when they go to the Net because they can't sleep.

The effect on the political process will be reinvigorating.

Chapter Nine

THE WEAKENING
OF POLITICAL PARTIES

ORIGINALLY, POLITICAL PARTIES were the instruments through which campaigns were waged. As this function has been usurped by television advertising, and soon will be further eroded by the Internet, political parties have had to cast about for a new role to play. Even the traditional function of parties as the arbiters of the nominating process has atrophied.

Since 1972, voters have taken away from political leaders the right to nominate candidates. The vast majority of candidates for Senate, House, governorship, mayoralty, or the state legislature are selected directly by the party's registered voters in primary elections. In many states Independents can vote in the primaries of an opposing party, and in some states any voter—even a member of an opposite party—can participate in primary elections.

The power of the party faithful to determine or even influence the selection of candidates has been substantially eroded.

In general elections, party loyalists are largely taken for granted. Typically, party candidates can count on more than 80 percent of their vote. Successful candidates spend much of their campaigns transcending party boundaries to appeal to the 40 percent of the electorate that has no party identification.

As political parties lost the ability to affect elections or even nominations, they defined a new role for themselves as fund-raisers and legislative arbiters. Even though they could no longer turn out the vote on election day, the partisan organization of Congress and the state legislatures let them influence the flow of legislation. Their ability to mobilize the party faithful gave them more ability than ever to marshal financial resources behind their candidates. These two functions—control of legislation and fundraising—offered national party structures an entree back into power.

Earlier in the century the situation was reversed. While political parties could still determine who was nominated and influence who was elected, they could do little to affect the flow of legislation. Between the late 1930s and the early 1970s, congressmen and senators routinely crossed party lines in their votes on bills. Indeed, the governing majority in both Houses during this forty-year period was a coalition of southern Democrats and conservative Republicans. Whichever party controlled Congress—usually it was the Democrats—the coalition wielded all the power.

Party lines meant little. Allegiance to the conservative coalition meant everything.

When the Civil Rights Act of 1964 passed, the prime goal of southern Democratic participation in the coalition—the frustration of racial integration—vanished. At about the same time, President Richard Nixon's southern strategy kicked in and the GOP came to challenge the formerly solid Democratic base in the South. As Republicans began their twenty-year march to dominance in southern politics, the "coalition" faded as a political factor in Congress and party lines reasserted themselves as the dominant force in determining how legislators voted. The final blow to the southern Democratic-Republican coalition was the erosion in the early and mid-'70s of the seniority system that determined committee assignments. Deprived of the power afforded by strict seniority, southern Democrats became an endangered species.

In the '80s and '90s, party loyalties became the determining factor in the passage of legislation. Senators and congressmen most often voted along party lines, with only a handful of conservative Democrats and moderate Republicans regularly crossing the gulf that separated them. The political party, deprived of power at the ballot box, acquired new clout as the arbiter of legislation.

As the relevance of party increased in Washington's corridors of power, special-interest groups began to ally with party leaders to promote the fortunes of candidates sympathetic to their points of view. Trial lawyers allied with Democrats, doctors with Republicans. Labor unions, Jewish groups, environmentalists, and gays backed Democrats while the Christian Coalition, the NRA, the National Federation of Small Businessmen, and the Chamber of Commerce stood with the GOP.

As interest groups picked sides, national party leaders came to have increased control over the spigot of campaign money. When special interests and their affiliated donors wanted to know whom they should fund to help their party take over the Senate or retain control of it, they called their party leaders. The parties became like artillery spotters, calling in fire in key Senate and congressional races throughout the country. Individual donors followed suit, checking with party leaders to figure out who needed money in races around the nation. Republicans organized Eagles' Clubs, groups of donors who agreed to give $1,000 (the legal maximum) to each of ten Senate races when party leaders asked for it.

Grown men and women actually wrote checks to fund candidates they not only had never met, but also had never even heard of. One imagines them asking the party honchos how to spell the names of those they were favoring with their largesse.

Stripped of electoral power, the political parties resumed their central role in our political process through their influence over legislation and over fundraising. But the Internet will weaken both sources of power and consign political parties to obscurity once more.

Voters, not political parties, will increasingly decide how members of Congress are to vote. Just as the electorate seized the power to nominate through direct primaries, their participation in Internet referendums will dominate how congressmen and senators come down on important issues. Legislators will no longer be able to toe the party line. Party will no longer be the principal factor in determining votes on legislation—the expressed views of the constituents will become the central issue.

Today congressmen and senators grit their teeth when the party calls and vote against the will of their district. Some are committed ideologues or even idealists who put their personal opinions well ahead of those of their constituents. They feel free to do so because they rely on massive campaign funding through the party to bail them out at election time. It is the certainty of access to money that fortifies their courage. They are confident that voters will forget their transgressions by election day and that they can swamp their opponents with television commercials.

The Internet will change both sides of this equation. On one side, it will make it harder for congressmen to vote against the will of their constituents. When a person votes in an accurate Internet referendum such as on Vote.com, the Web site will keep track of his vote and advise him of how his congressman votes when the issue comes up in Congress. Those who disregard the opinions of their electorate will pay a heavy price on election day. On the other side of the equation, the Internet will reduce the importance of fundraising and make the allure of party or special-interest money much less attractive. It will cost a congressman a high political price to march to the beat of the special-interest or party drummer, and the rewards for doing so will be decreasingly important.

As political parties lose their ability to control how Congress votes, and find their capacity to raise funds diminished, their power will atrophy. Both the Democratic and Republican organizations will begin to fade from prominence in a nation of largely Independent voters. Political parties, having already lost control of the nominating and electoral process, will now find their powers further reduced and will resume their well-deserved march toward irrelevance.

Ultimately, for the political parties to achieve relevance in the new age of Fifth Estate politics, they will have to establish Web sites of their own to feature and showcase their candidates, issues, and campaigns. The ability of parties to attract voters to their sites and get them to click on the sites of those whom they are promoting for public office could be crucial to their ability to make it in the new era of Internet politics. If political parties can perform some kind of mediating role by aggregating voters on their Web sites and then giving them information about the local candidates for each office (perhaps in response to a zip-code prompt entered by the voter), candidates will again find it useful to compete for the favor of party leaders.

Chapter Ten

THE LOBBYISTS MEET
DEMOCRACY

WILLIE SUTTON SAID he robbed banks because "that's where the money is." Lobbyists have to go where the power is. In the era of the Fourth Estate it was in the legislative halls. Working the corridors of power—literally the lobbies—is how special-interest pleaders got their name. With the rise of the Fifth Estate, the locus of power will shift and lobbyists will have to adjust their focus to fit these changing times. Instead of lobbying them—the elected officials who hold positions in Congress—they will have to spend more of their time lobbying us—those who will dominate Congress by speaking out over the Internet.

When narrow special-interest issues arise, the old ways of lobbying will still prove effective. Internet referendums will not be able to offer guidance on the minutiae of the tax code or on special appropriations for this or that interest group. But on the high-visibility issues like Fast Track trade legislation, NAFTA ratification, welfare reform, Social Security, the uses of the budget surplus, abortion, and other central questions, it is the will of the people, as expressed over the Internet, that will hold the balance of power.

As they have come to recognize the power of public opinion, special-interest groups are increasingly trying to reach a general audience. While the majority still try to influence public policy the old way—with campaign contributions and golf games with legislators—a new breed of special interests has focused on galvanizing their memberships into political action, seeking to use their power of numbers and noise to sway Congress or state legislatures.

Unfortunately, the pioneer in these efforts has been the National Rifle Association. Over the years, understanding how unpopular is their affection for automatic weapons, the NRA has become incredibly skilled at using its members as a political tool. Unlike many special-interest groups, the NRA doesn't even aspire to popularity. When it seeks to influence an election, it doesn't advertise on television or radio. Instead, the NRA sends mailings to its members to urge them to vote for their favored candidates in elections. The NRA emphasizes its capacity to turn out a disciplined bloc of voters for or against any candidate to strike terror into the hearts of wavering congressmen and senators when gun-control legislation comes up for a vote.

Taking a page from their book, other relatively unpopular interest groups, trial lawyers for example, have taken to using television and radio ads to emphasize their views and win adherents among the electorate. But most special-interest groups focus their main energies on lobbying members of Congress the old-fashioned way, with donations and whispers in their ears.

Labor unions, once the very essence of grassroots organization, have so lost touch with their own members that they are today little more than pension funds with political-action committees. With a largely captive membership base, they realize that they cannot effectively mobilize their supporters and must rely on their ability to fund campaigns of compliant Democrats in order to be heard in the legislative halls. To preserve their dignity, unions maintain the fiction that they speak for their members and can mobilize them when needed, but most professionals know this is mainly bluff and bluster.

The fact is that elections are an inconvenience to most lobbyists and special-interest groups. Satisfied with their current web of relationships, they see change as threatening to the cozy networks of support and influence they have spent years cultivating. By far the largest share of special-interest campaign donations goes to incumbents through their political-action committees. Only a tiny share funds insurgents.

Currying favor with the Fifth Estate, special interests and lobbyists will succeed or fail based on their ability to move ordinary people to log on and vote their way in Internet referendums. The special interests will have to become much better at influencing public opinion if they are to remain relevant to the political process.

Few elected officials will have the courage to defy the expressed will of their own constituents even if campaign donations beckon them to do so.

Initially, membership organizations, such as the NRA, will have especial clout. Those organizations that can generate millions of Internet votes will have an edge over groups that are essentially just fundraising and lobbying operations. For example, trial lawyers currently enjoy an advantage over doctors in their constant fighting over medical malpractice legislation. Able to generate funds from other members of the bar, trial lawyers, per capita, far out-contribute doctors in this perennial battle. But with the Fifth Estate, the doctors, superior in numbers, will enjoy the edge.

Groups like the NRA, the National Federation of Small Businessmen, and the Christian Coalition will do much better in presenting their case because of their ability to tap into their substantial grassroots organizations. Labor unions, on the other hand, out of touch with their memberships, will find it harder and harder to lobby effectively.

Increasingly though, even membership organizations will find that Internet voting overtakes them. While groups like the NRA and the Christian Coalition can turn out millions of members to vote in Internet referendums, the views they represent are still alien to the vast bulk of the electorate. Most voters, by good-sized margins, support gun control and legal access to abortion. Ultimately, the ability of right-wing interest groups to mobilize their members will be dwarfed as the average voter makes his or her opinion felt on the Net. As not millions, but tens of millions, log on and vote in Internet referendums, this increased turnout will overtake the ability of special-interest membership organizations to turn out the vote.

The efforts of the health insurance industry that led to the defeat of the Clinton healthcare reform program will have to become more of the prototype for lobbying in the new era. As the insurance companies funded massive advertising to undermine voter support for Hillary Clinton's reforms, and the tobacco companies used advertising to kill a proposed raise in tobacco taxes in 1998, so those who seek to move Congress will first have to move the voters.

But even these financial powerhouses will ultimately be overtaken by the revolution of the Fifth Estate. Their ability to fund big campaigns will matter less and less as the very impact of advertising and money declines while Internet use rises and broadcast-television viewership drops. Just as money will matter less in electing politicians, it will also matter less in persuading voters.

Eventually the big winners in Fifth Estate lobbying will be the public-interest groups. Their capacity to appeal to the average voter will count for a lot. Groups like the Sierra Club, the Audubon Society, the Public Interest Research Group, and Common Cause have never been big donors to political candidates. Their strength lies in the appeal of their issues and the attractiveness of their arguments. In the Internet era, they will be able to manifest the broad support their issues enjoy without having to donate millions of dollars to candidates running for office. In the era of the Fifth Estate, the special interests will find it harder to get their will implemented while public-interest groups will have a field day.

As special interests struggle to compete, they will find that they have to modify their positions to make them more attractive to ordinary voters. Only in states with referendums and popular-initiative laws do these political behemoths have to cater to public opinion. While they are often able to defeat good legislation by blitzing the electorate with television ads, the ability of voters in referendum states to pass good laws far outstrips that of state legislatures to do so where referendums are not permitted.

The Internet will ultimately prove to be a great leveler in the process of influencing legislation.

In the new world of Internet politics, the political glue that holds coalitions together will be the interaction between Web sites. The Sierra Club Web site will run a page of banner ads each of which, when clicked, sends the visitor to the Web sites of candidates whom they favor. All other interest groups, from the American Association of Retired Persons (AARP) to the National Rifle Association, will do likewise.

In the past, interest groups measured their political clout by boasting of hundreds of thousands of members or of a huge bank account to use in donations to candidates. Now special-interest groups that are able to get lots of Internet visitors will have a virtual constituency that they can encourage to click on to a candidate's Web site to his political advantage. Any group with such a site will be a Goliath in the Internet campaign process.

How will the most powerful special-interest groups fare in this competition? The large memberships of some organizations, like the NRA or the Christian Coalition, will undoubtedly make their Web sites popular destinations among their rank and file. But how useful will these visitors be in catalyzing a candidacy? Since most are already strong supporters of their organizations, it is unlikely that the visitors will include a lot of Independent or undecided voters.

Labor unions have a somewhat different problem. They have large membership bases, but unlike the NRA and the Christian Coalition, their members are not always committed to the candidates their leaders support. The problem labor will have is getting large numbers of less-educated workers to use the Internet in the first place. If the unions can get their members interested in their Web sites, the ongoing communication can do a great deal to restore labor's waning political power.

The American Association of Retired Persons, another powerful lobbying force, also faces the problem of teaching its elderly members to use the Internet. But as seniors catch on and log on, the AARP will likely be a political powerhouse in Internet politics.

Trial lawyers seem most likely to suffer, since they have neither a large membership base nor access to a constituency. Their salvation would have to be in generating a Web site with interesting and important information and legal advice that would attract a great number of interested visitors.

Public-interest groups, such as environmental, consumer, and education organizations, may be the big winners in the Web-site age. Their ability to post interesting and attractive data on their Web sites to bring in millions of browsers could give them a capacity to reach their constituents, which their limited financial clout now denies them.

Constrained by limited budgets, how are groups like the Ozone Action Coalition to reach the tens of millions of Americans who are deeply concerned about global warming? By mail or phone, the costs would be prohibitive. Advertising on any large scale is well beyond their means. But their access to interesting information may make their Web site a popular destination that environmentally conscious voters seek out on their own initiative. The resulting ability to speak to swing voters will give these groups tremendous new power.

·   ·   ·

As money means less in the political process, corporations will be less able to buy their way to political power. Companies with a mjor role in the Internet, like America Online, Yahoo, Excite, and Amazon.com, will have special political power. Since they attract millions to their Web sites each day, they can play a huge role as arbiters of our political process by granting candidates access to their home pages. In Internet campaigning, the equivalent of a free ad on a prime-time TV show will be a banner atop the AOL home page.

Of course, in politics "free media" isn't free. Campaign finance reform provides each candidate with a certain amount of free media time, but it still costs money to hire issues experts, publicists, writers, and creative talent. These costs are, however, minor compared with the gargantuan price of television advertising.

But how will election finance regulators count this in-kind contribution from cybercorporations? Will they limit or ban it? Will they require equal access for all candidates? How will that work? Will Internet companies be required to maintain the same impartiality and offer similarly nonpartisan access as television networks and radio stations now must do? Or will they be allowed to help a candidate whom they favor? These are the crucial questions of campaign regulation down the road.

Chapter Eleven

STATE AND LOCAL POLITICS

THE REVOLUTION THAT Internet voting will bring to the federal government will also soon make itself felt at the state and local levels.

Today most state legislatures are notoriously insensitive to the will of their constituents. Many, like the one in New York, have zealously resisted giving voters the right to petition to put initiatives on the ballot. They insist on monopolizing the legislative process and they hoard their power, fearing to turn it over to their own electorate. But these politicians will find, to their dismay, that voters will seize that right to make their own decisions through the Internet, just as they will do in national politics.

Voters will log on to Web sites like Vote.com to participate in referendums not only on federal issues but also on state and local matters. They will demand the same attention to their views from state legislatures and city councils that they ask of Congress. But the battle to bring accountability to state and local legislative bodies will be far more difficult than it is to wring this responsiveness from Congress.

In many states, the legislatures are in the grip of powerful political machines that have long defied public opinion. In New York, for example, there is virtually no involuntary turnover in the state legislature. It is easier to get a protected civil-service worker like a police officer or a tenured teacher fired than it is to defeat a member of the New York State Legislature who wants to be reelected. Those who seek out vacancies would do better to read the obituaries than the news pages of the paper to find them.

A big part of the relative invulnerability of state legislators stems from a simple fact: they draw their own lines for their legislative districts. Members of the U.S. Senate have to run statewide. House of Representatives candidates have to stand for election in districts drawn for them by their respective state legislatures. But members of local state legislatures get to draw the lines themselves. Every ten years, following the census, members of local legislatures scramble to cut deals to draw district lines that assure them of a long tenure in office. In the made-to-order districts that emerge from this corrupted process, they succeed in guaranteeing lifetime tenure.

State legislators are also less vulnerable to defeat because voters know less about them. Events in Congress are widely reported throughout the media, but in many states there is very limited reporting of what goes on in the state legislature.

In states where the capital is the largest city—Arkansas, Massachusetts, Arizona, Mississippi, Georgia, North Carolina, Tennessee, Indiana, and Iowa—the media pays much more attention to the workings of state government. In these states, the media closely covers state politics and reports on its activities as extensively as it does on local or mayoral issues. The proximity of the news organ's base of operations to the center of the state's political activity catalyzes a level of coverage of state government that is typically extensive.

But in most states things are different because the capital city and the largest city in the state are different. Voters in Pittsburgh or Philadelphia don't get to hear much about what happens in Harrisburg, the state capital. The New York City press corps does a very poor job of covering what is going on in the state government based in Albany. In cities like Chicago, Detroit, Cleveland, Cincinnati, St. Louis, Kansas City, Los Angeles, San Francisco, Houston, or Dallas, there is relatively little coverage of state politics since the capital is located elsewhere.

The net effect is that in many parts of the country the voters don't know very much about their state government, compared with the extraordinary levels of information they get about local or national politics. As a result of this dearth of news coverage, state legislatures have been able to avoid really representing the will of their voters. The growth of national cable news stations and the decreasing ratings of local broadcast news shows also influences this growing disparity between the amount people know about national as opposed to state government. There is of course no C-SPAN, no *Newsweek* or *Time* magazines, and no CNN or Fox News Channel aimed at state or local government in most major media markets.

State legislatures are notorious for their control by special-interest groups. Typically, the party's majority or minority leader in each chamber of the legislature raises a very large percentage of the money available to their members as they run for reelection. The easiest and most ready source of money is special-interest groups whose lobbyists hang around the state capital like flies at a picnic. Interest groups such as trial lawyers, doctors, farmers, bankers, insurance agents, manufacturers, casino owners, and the like so dominate political fundraising for state legislators that their influence runs deep.

As a direct result of the power the party leaders have over fundraising, most state legislatures cast party-line votes most of the time. For all the power that national political parties have in Washington, it is very rare for all Democrats to vote one way and all Republicans to vote the other. But in state legislatures it is common. In fact, in the New York State Legislature, votes are usually cast by what is called the "short roll call." In this procedure, the majority leader votes first and the minority leader votes next. No other members vote. All other legislators are presumed to vote the way their party leader did unless they specifically rise to "switch" their votes.

This combination of limited information to the public, party-line discipline, special-interest money, and the ability to control redistricting is deadly to democracy at the state level. State legislatures are often so deeply entrenched that it matters little what voters think. Again to cite an example from New York State, the Democratic Party has controlled the lower House, the state assembly, ever since 1974 while the Republicans have controlled the upper chamber, the state senate, since the mid-'60s. They march to the beat of their party leaders' drums with little real concern for what the voters in their districts think. And they get away with it.

In frustration, voters in many states have pushed for procedures to crack the control of their state legislatures by special interests and party machines. Many regularly use referendums or voter initiatives to keep their legislatures honest. Others have pushed through term limits that force incumbents to vacate their offices after several terms.

The fact that voters have adopted these measures to circumvent their state legislatures shows the depth of the public's frustration at their inability to be heard by those who should represent them.

So much for the give-and-take of democracy.

But Internet voting will likely change all that in the future. By transcending the limited space of newspapers or TV news broadcasts, the Internet will increasingly cover state and local news effectively and intimately. As the idea of Internet referendums works its way down to the state and local levels, voters will become better informed about what their legislators are doing. As the public learns more about what is going on in their state capital, they are not likely to take kindly to watching their ideas disregarded and their thoughts ignored.

The irresistible force—an electorate aroused by the power of its new Internet voice—will meet the immovable object: the political machines that run most state legislatures. Eventually the voters will have their way and the state legislatures will have to pay vastly more attention to the views of those they allegedly represent. Party leaders will find that their ability to command the absolute loyalty of their state representatives and state senators will be eroded and special interests will find local legislative bodies harder than ever to control.

There will be an outbreak of democracy at the state and local level that will do much to reinvigorate democracy at all levels of government. Especially on the local or municipal level, the Internet democracy will reduce the gap between those who are elected and those they represent. It will give voters a new capacity to influence the decisions at the local level that affect their lives the most. The voters' intimacy with the issues that dominate most local politics will provide an especial impetus to Internet participation when people realize that it offers them a new tool to shape their communities. When local referendums are held over the Net on zoning and land-use issues, for example, the alienation between the governed and the government will decrease. Even if members of the zoning board don't see the harm in the massive housing development proposed for the only remaining vacant land in the municipality, the voters are likely to think otherwise.

Internet voting will seriously challenge the hubris of local, town, and city officials who make decisions for their communities without consultation. Do we really need the new stadium? Should this company get a tax abatement so it will stay in town? How will we handle the increased traffic if we approve the new shopping center? These decisions may continue to be made by political leaders who would disregard our views. But it will be harder for them to ignore us when tens of thousands of local residents express the desire over the Internet to reverse their decisions. It will be even harder for them to explain, in the next election, why they paid no attention when we spoke.

Chapter Twelve

HOW THE INTERNET WILL CHANGE THE JUSTICE SYSTEM

JUST AS THE INTERNET will dramatically change how the executive and legislative branches function, so it will bring huge changes to the judiciary.

For members of the Fifth Estate, important litigation will be played out on an interactive public stage. Tens of millions of Internet users will be as involved as if they were actually sitting in the courtroom as members of a jury. Some witnesses will have been cross-examined in public before they ever see the inside of a courtroom.

While today it is commonplace for pretrial publicity to lead us to premature conclusions over the guilt or innocence of the defendant, the intrusion of the Internet into the process of judgment will be even more profound in the future. As virtual juries follow the play-by-play of the court proceedings online, they will vote on the credibility of each witness as his testimony unfolds. Like a giant focus group, they will suffuse the atmosphere with their views and reactions.

Trials today are often conducted amid a circus of media attention. But at least today the public doesn't talk back. While polls gauge public opinion about the innocence or guilt of a figure standing trial, these measurements are episodic and blunt instruments compared with the precision of feedback in the Internet era.

Did the judge rule correctly in not permitting a certain piece of evidence to come in? Was the eyewitness credible? How did the defense attorney do in his closing argument? Internet Web sites will pose each of these issues and millions will vote on them.

Everything about important trials will be up for grabs on the Internet. Lawyers will monitor Internet reactions as the trial unfolds, just as politicians keep their eyes on each night's tracking polls to test the effectiveness of each speech or advertisement. Law firms might well underwrite virtual trials, in advance, on the Internet to learn how to tailor their presentations for maximum effectiveness.

This growth of popular control of the judicial process through the Internet is deeply disturbing. The intrusion of direct popular participation into the spheres traditionally reserved for politics is healthy. It is democracy at work. But nobody supposes that democracy is the right way to run a criminal justice system. The Internet could well lead to interactive kangaroo courts or a popular lynch-mob psychology that would be wholly destructive to our system of trial by jury and the presumption of innocence that rests at its base.

While most of the changes likely to be brought about by the Fifth Estate are salutary, this one is not. Indeed, the whole capacity of our justice system to operate without fear or favor may well be in peril.

We began to see this politicization of the judicial process most clearly during the unimpeachment as President Clinton used the powers and techniques of politics to survive the attempt to remove him from office.

One by one, the women of Clinton's life came out of the closet to reveal their secrets. No sooner did they speak out in public than they found themselves defamed, discredited, and on the defensive.

Initially, the victims of Clinton's revenge arguably deserved some kind of rebuttal. Gennifer Flowers, with whom Clinton eventually admitted having had an affair, broadcast her story for money in the sleazy *Star* magazine and posed nude in *Penthouse* magazine to bring publicity to her accusations. Called a "gold digger" by Clinton apologists and derided by Hillary as a "cabaret lounge singer," this former TV reporter went through the ringer as the Clinton damage-control team savaged her in public. It is one of the colossal mysteries of all time how she came to be disbelieved even though she had tapes that clearly showed her intimacy with candidate Bill Clinton.

So obvious was it that she was telling the truth that Clinton defenders later cited the Flowers episode to say that we'd had warning of the low moral character of our future president when we voted for him and his philandering should have come as no surprise. Their defense rather reminded one of the case put forth by tobacco companies that opposed victim suits citing warning labels on packages to show that their customers knew cigarettes caused cancer when they smoked them.

But as the unimpeachment unfolded, Clinton's tactic of defaming witnesses and dismissing their wrath was visited not just on those who came forward for profit. The president's team equally sought to destroy women who testified under subpoena, unwillingly and under threat of perjury. Apparently the president did not realize that only he could escape punishment for lying under oath.

· · ·

In an earlier time the FBI might have been used to unearth compromising material on presidential opponents. Digging up dirt is nothing new. But what is new, and what the president and his people used so masterfully, is the multiplicity of news and Internet outlets that are willing to run smear stories and the ease with which they enter the journalistic bloodstream from there. These accusations of misconduct, directed against private citizens, were not just whispered into a few knowing ears. They were broadcast throughout the land and became common knowledge among vast numbers of ordinary Americans. How any of these people can resume their normal lives now that their private lives have been trumpeted all the world over is hard to imagine.

The legacy of intimidation that Clinton leaves behind him will go so far as to undermine the free-speech guarantees of the First Amendment when it comes to criticizing the personal behavior of a president. It's true that nobody will be thrown in prison for attesting to sex or other illicit activity with a president, but the injury to the person's character that will surely follow makes the right to speak out largely theoretical.

.   .   .

But visualize the scenario of the unimpeachment as it might have played out in the era of the Internet. Each day, millions of Web users would vote on whether they believed Kathleen Willey or whether they felt that Juanita Broderick was telling the truth when she said Clinton had raped her. The results would shape how we regarded their testimony even more than polling does today.

Nowhere are the new rules of Fifth Estate trials more dramatically in evidence than in the war between Bill Clinton and Kenneth Starr. The president defeated the prosecutor because, while the chief executive was playing under Fifth Estate rules, the independent counsel was following the guidelines of the Fourth Estate.

To the Fourth Estate, prosecutors and judges were traditionally outside of politics. Even when they had to stand for election, they were usually treated with deference and respect. From their lofty perches they were mostly able to ignore public opinion and concentrate on their duties. But Bill Clinton realized that, as far as the Fifth Estate is concerned, nobody is above politics. We insist on the right to judge everybody. To Clinton, Special

Prosecutor Kenneth Starr was just another political opponent, the latest in a long series. Playing under Fourth Estate rules, Kenneth Starr saw the judges and juries he would face as his audience. Bill Clinton knew the real power lay with public opinion. As Clinton's lawyers strung out the probe by every possible procedural motion, his press people blamed Starr for the delays that eventuated. Americans came to believe that Starr was consumed by an ideological and almost pathological desire to get Bill Clinton. Starr's ratings had sunk so low that he couldn't win a case before the Senate or even a jury. The prosecutor had been prosecuted in the court of public opinion, found guilty, and sentenced to impotence.

When first Napoleon and then Hitler invaded Russia, they each won virtually every battle. The Russian army reeled backwards, retreating through the endless Russian steppes, burning villages and destroying crops and cattle as they withdrew. Soon the invaders' supply lines were stretched so thin that their inability to locate sustenance in the towns and villages they occupied crippled them and extinguished their momentum. While the invaders tried to stab Russia through the heart, the Russians counterattacked in the stomach.

These are the same tactics that Clinton used to defeat Kenneth Starr.

Clinton's lawyers, like the Russian generals, fought a series of losing battles over every kind of privilege imaginable. They lost all but one of these claims. Each defeat was appealed and each appeal led to another defeat. Starr won them all. But as the clock

kept ticking, public patience with the length of Starr's investigation wore thin. Like the Russians destroying their crops as they
retreated, the White House used each assertion of privilege to
paint Starr as a prosecutor out of control, a modern equivalent of
Inspector Javert in *Les Misérables* or of Captain Ahab in *Moby Dick*,
obsessed with catching his quarry. Each time Starr's and Clinton's
lawyers exchanged legal briefs, Clinton's media experts released
press statements attacking the special prosecutor. They would
always point out how long Starr had been investigating Clinton
and how much money he had spent, blithely ignoring that it was
Clinton's motions and Clinton's tactics that caused both the
delays and the costs. Clinton lost on the law, but Starr earned
only the impatience of the American people.

Kenneth Starr, who perhaps resembled Peter Sellers' Inspector
Clouseau more than Victor Hugo's Inspector Javert, never knew
what was happening to him. A lawyer, a former judge, and a prosecutor, he paid attention only to events on the legal playing field,
ignoring what was going on in the stands. When he had finally
forced every last witness to testify and disposed of every fictitious
privilege asserted by the White House lawyers, he was left with a
proven legal case and an unwinnable political one. In a courtroom, he might have won. But before the Senate, he lost.

Likely as a result of White House prodding, the Secret Service
refused to let their agents testify about what they observed while
protecting the president. The District Court overruled them.
Undaunted, Clinton appealed and lost again. Finally the Supreme

Court had to rule against the claim of privilege in order for the agents to testify. The agent testimony hurt Clinton, but the months and months of delay caused by the White House motions hurt Starr more.

Similarly, White House lawyers argued that presidential aide Sidney Blumenthal should not be required to testify on the grounds of executive privilege. Again, the White House lost at every turn. But once more Starr was blamed for the delay.

Starr never realized that the rules had changed. In the emerging Fifth Estate, the court that mattered was public opinion. He was mired in a popularity contest with an elected president. Only one man would emerge with his reputation and it would not necessarily be the one who was right or who proved his case. It would be the one who was left standing after the slugfest had run its course.

The White House may have been outclassed legally, but Starr was hopelessly outclassed politically. By the time his impeachment recommendations landed on the desks of the House Judiciary Committee, the prosecutor had become the investigation's biggest liability.

Clinton has shown himself to be a master of the Fifth Estate rules where everybody is in politics once they are in the public eye, whether they like it or not. You run against a prosecutor just as you run against an opposing candidate, with polling, negative research, and public attacks. Everybody is fair game.

Chapter Thirteen

INTERNATIONAL DEMOCRACY

THE INTERNET KNOWS no national boundaries. Its reach effortlessly spans oceans, mountains, frontiers, and ideologies.

Though the Chinese have tried, no totalitarian regime can control access to the Internet if the computer and the telephone are sufficiently widespread. A fundamental contradiction bedevils dictatorships in our modern age—you can't develop your economy without widespread use of computers and you can't control informational flows if those computers are accessible.

Today, Internet use is highly concentrated in the United States. For the moment, the implications of Internet voting and democracy will, therefore, be mostly felt in the fifty states. But when the Internet expands in other nations, it will trigger major political changes. The following chart summarizes the extent of Internet use in the various nations of the world:

INTERNET USE BY COUNTRY

Nation	Number of Weekly Internet Users (in Millions)
UNITED STATES	77
JAPAN	10
UNITED KINGDOM	8
GERMANY	7
CANADA	6
AUSTRALIA	4
FRANCE	3
SWEDEN	3
TAIWAN	2
SOUTH KOREA	2
SPAIN	2
NETHERLANDS	2
CHINA	2
FINLAND	2

For now, the United States dominates the world of the Net. Japan, whose ten million users earn it second place among the nations of the world in Internet use, has a population half that of the U.S., yet its Internet use is only one-eighth as much.

Obviously, this situation will change. Just as the automobile and the airplane began to come into common use in the United States and then spread throughout the globe, so Internet use will surely proliferate in other nations.

The implications of Internet use are even more dramatic for foreign countries than they are for the United States. Flawed as it may be, the United States is the most democratic nation on earth. Even other democracies offer their people far less power and consult with them less intensively and less frequently than we do in the U.S. Civil liberties are much more limited even in nations like Britain and France. State and local governments typically have much less power or citizen participation.

France, for example, has a weak system of local government. All major decisions are made by the central government. This lack of local power has even been a major factor in the spread of nuclear power throughout the country. Where local opposition checked the expansion of nuclear energy in parts of Western Europe and in much of the United States, the French people had no recourse but to sit by and watch nuclear cooling towers spring up all along the banks of their beautiful Rhone, Seine, and Loire rivers.

When the Internet becomes more widespread in France, it is a safe bet that people will let the members of the Chamber of Deputies know, through Internet voting, what they think about issues like these. As in the United States, the political power that the people are denied will be seized through Internet referendums.

No nation in the world has a system of initiative and referendum quite like that in many states of our nation. The rest of the world is not prepared for this level of popular consultation and the constant intrusion of frequent expressions of popular will. The democracies of the world are in for a shock. No longer will French farmers have to blockade the roads, or Italian workers go on strike, to be heard. Their demands will go forth electronically over the Net. On the other hand, when they exceed the bounds of public sympathy, the spines of elected officials will doubtless be stiffened by the popular consultation the Internet will make possible.

As the European Union continues down the path of continental integration, the Internet will likely afford a mechanism for a continent-wide expression of views that will be in place long before the various sovereign nations see fit to surrender political control to a joint government. With a speed that will far outstrip the ponderous pace of political integration and the slow dissolution of national sovereignty, technology will fashion a European electorate whose voice will transcend the timid and halting steps of its national leaders toward unity. We will hear the voice of Europe over the Internet long before we hear it from any official organ. The Internet will give Europe its voice long before the ballot box does.

Who can speculate about the impact of the Internet in autocratic nations like China? Now, while a handful of people has access to the Net, the government puts people in jail for Internet use. But when the need for economic growth forces more widespread use of computers and the Internet, how will Beijing be able to keep them down on the farm? According to the research firm Computer Economics, as reported by ABC News, China will have thirty-seven million Internet users by 2005. Can one imagine millions or tens of millions of Chinese voting over the

Internet on issues about which their government refuses to consult them? Will the day come when Internet users in Beijing and Shanghai will register their opinions of the decisions taken behind closed doors about who will lead their nation?

Countries where tyranny is less pronounced and less reprehensible than in China will find that their people can become embarrassingly outspoken over the Internet. The ongoing informal consultation that Internet voting will inevitably bring to their societies will cause fundamental shifts in influence and power.

Undemocratic governments will find themselves embarrassed by Internet voting that reflects popular impatience or disagreement with their policies. How would Serbian lawlessness in the Balkans have been curbed if the people of Yugoslavia could vote, without government permission, on the brutal, expansionist policy of Milosevic? What impetus would there have been toward the peace process in places like Ireland and Israel if Internet voting had allowed the people to be heard on the side of nonviolence and accommodation?

Sometimes of course people are wrong. In many cases Internet voting will underscore the failure of leaders to bring about the consent and agreement of those they allegedly represent. But that's the nature of democracy.

Chapter Fourteen

THE EMPIRE STRIKES BACK

THE POWER STRUCTURE will not give way lightly to the rule of the Internet. The Fourth Estate will not welcome the Fifth.

Initially the Establishment media will ignore Internet democracy. They will be very slow to report the emergence of the Internet as a political power and will accord little importance to its pronouncements. Internet voting can expect to be disparaged and largely ignored by the media just as talk radio has been.

Call-in political radio, another driving force in the emerging American direct democracy, is largely ignored by the Establishment media. Even though Rush Limbaugh broadcasts on 650 radio stations and claims a weekly listening audience of over twenty million Americans, his name appears in the *New York Times* only occasionally. He was mentioned just thirty-three times in all of 1998 and thirty-nine times in all of 1997, mostly in minor articles that attracted little attention, even though he broadcasts to more than one in ten American adults each week.

In its early days, the voting over Web sites like Vote.com will likely be derided as inaccurate or susceptible to fraud. The media Establishment will belittle the Internet referendums as unrepresentative of the general public. Pollsters will attack the results of the referendums as being distorted by the upscale and young demographics of Internet use.

When the Vote.com Web site sponsors its presidential primary, the Establishment will do its best to ignore it. Even though the media attaches great importance to the symbolic votes of twenty-five thousand picnickers at the Republican Party's summer outing in Iowa, they will not pay much attention to the Internet presidential primary, which will likely attract many more participants, even in Iowa alone.

But the politicians will get the point. Votes are votes. Soon the political field of candidates and the hallways of the Senate and the House will move under the influence of the Internet voting process. When the Internet begins to affect how these political figures vote and what they say, the Establishment media will have no choice but to cover it and report on the activities of their Fifth Estate rivals.

Then the war will start. Fourth Estate leaders will warn of the demagogic potential of the Internet referendums and will lament the death of principle in the rise of popular democracy. Ignoring the more pernicious influence of special interests and their campaign contributions on the deliberations of Congress, they will wring their hands at the onset of so unbridled a power as the massive, spontaneous expressions of public will over the Internet. As its creator, the government will seek to limit the Net and impose various constraints upon it.

The most obvious of these will be attempts at censorship under the guise of protecting public morals and decency. While it is hard to imagine a more pornographic moment in American history than the Clinton impeachment trial, legislators will bemoan the easy access to cybersex over the Net and will worry that a new generation is about to be led astray. Their efforts to limit access to the Net or to fight porn sites may well spill over into efforts to chill participation in political dialogue.

·   ·   ·

The second front in the Establishment's effort to limit the power of the Internet will concern tax policy. With $300 billion in e-commerce in 1998, state and local governments are demanding the power to tax Internet sales. Despite huge budget surpluses in most states, the local bureaucrats cannot stand the diversion of commerce away from sales-taxable channels. While they make a reasonable case for sales taxation of e-commerce, the chances are that sales taxes will merely pave the way for more general taxes on Internet use. That which is now free will be taxed so that government can control it. The power to tax is the power to destroy, as the Supreme Court articulated in the *Marbury v. Madison* case. The danger is that a benign and good-faith effort to tax e-commerce will spill over into broader taxation of the Net.

Finally, the Establishment will seek to deny to the Internet the free speech protections accorded other forms of publication. In the recent libel suit brought by White House aide Sidney Blumenthal against Internet reporter Matt Drudge, U.S. District Court Judge Paul Freidman refused to extend the same free-speech protection to Drudge that covers more conventional journalists. The *New York Times* reported that "in allowing the suit against Drudge to stand, the judge called the commentator 'simply a purveyor of gossip'" who had no right to the libel protections enjoyed by legitimate journalists. Drudge replied with a confession that "I am not a journalist. I am a kangaroo."

The position of the court is plainly ridiculous. If the spoken word is a protected form of publication under the First Amendment, why shouldn't it be protected when tapped out on a computer keyboard? This blind spot in the court's ruling is just an example of the Establishment's reticence to accept the Internet as the new frontier in journalism.

None of these threats is likely to cripple the headlong rush of the Internet into new forms of democracy. The fact is that there is little anyone can do to deny voters the outlets that technology affords them for expressing their opinions. Internet democracy is here to stay. There is only one force on earth that can deny it— a collective reappraisal by the average Internet user of the wisdom of a fully responsive direct democracy.

Chapter Fifteen

THE INEVITABLE BACKLASH

WINSTON CHURCHILL SAID that democracy was "the worst form of government, except for all the others." The problem with democracy is that people are wrong . . . a lot. As Internet voting amplifies their often ill-considered views and lends extra force to their prejudices of the moment, the control rod of representative democracy will be less able to contain destructive passions than it has ever been before.

Had we listened to democracy, we probably would never have declared independence from England, abolished slavery, or armed Europe in World War II before Pearl Harbor forced us into the war. Democracy supported McCarthyism for a long, long time. There is no telling how far public opinion would have backed racism and reaction in the silent-majority days of Richard Nixon. Repeatedly, the Supreme Court has had to draw the line against infringements of free speech, the free press, and the rights of criminal defendants.

If we had a pure democracy, we would likely end up with no democracy.

Inevitably, Internet voting will lead to a backlash as people come to appreciate their own mistakes. Fifteen years from now, people will likely say that the pendulum has swung too far away from listening to our elected officials and too much toward direct popular democracy. As the evidence mounts that people have made wrong choices and voted their fears and hates more than their hopes and dreams, we will collectively come to realize the need to curb ourselves and bring back the system of checks and balances so basic to our Constitution.

The time will come when we voluntarily relinquish some, but certainly not all, of the power we will have acquired through Internet voting and return to the Hamiltonian ideal of listening to those who are better informed and better educated than we are.

It is not unheard of for a democracy to cede its powers to experts. In fact, in America it happens all the time. Consider two examples: the unprecedented grant of almost total power over our economy to the Federal Reserve Board and the hands-off posture of the commander in chief on military operations.

Before the Clinton administration, Fed bashing was a traditional pastime both at the White House and in Congress. Presidents routinely criticized the Fed for maintaining too tight a rein on the money supply and for failing to cut interest rates for fear of inflation. President Clinton gnashed his teeth in private during much of 1995 and 1996, hoping the Fed would cut rates to permit the economy to grow its way out of the budget deficit without the need for wrenching cuts. But he kept his silence in public. When he briefly considered appointing Felix Rohayten to the Fed Board because of his pro-growth policies, he resisted the temptation and named Alice Rivlin—a certified inflation fighter—instead. The policy at the Clinton White House was clear: no Fed bashing, no matter what!

Feisty Texas populist Congressman Wright Patman used to inveigh against the Federal Reserve Board with the same passion that Andrew Jackson brought to his opposition to the Bank of the United States in the early nineteenth century. Regularly congressmen would threaten to cut the power of the Fed through legislation. Fed Chairmen Volker and Greenspan had to submit to the indignity of relatively harsh questioning in their appearances before congressional committees. But no more. Now the senators and congressmen listen in respectful silence as the Fed chairman spins his web. Greenspan, whose reputation for clarity of language is exceeded only by that of former baseball manager Casey Stengel, can get away with oblique references and veiled allusions without having to lay his cards on the table. The oracle of Apollo at Delphi never got such rapt attention.

After Vietnam, the consensus developed that generals should run the military and that politicians should butt out. After Lyndon Johnson micromanaged the war in Vietnam, choosing targets for the nightly bombing raids and regularly overruling his generals, both Presidents Reagan and Bush declared a hands-off policy on military action. Once the order to go in was issued, they both left the operations in the hands of the military. Except for some interference during the Kosovo operation to limit military and civilian casualties, President Clinton has continued this tradition. Doubtless motivated in part by his own well-publicized lack of military experience, Clinton has sought to remove himself from the day-to-day control of military operations to which his job as commander in chief entitles him.

Just as we have ceded power to the experts over such vital areas of our nation's life as the economy and the military, so Internet voting will eventually lead to a national consensus that the people have too much power and that it would be wiser to listen to those who have more information and wisdom. But this conclusion will not come until Internet democracy has had its full chance and the people have overcome decades of pent-up frustration at the special-interest domination and partisanship of Congress. Like the French Revolutionaries seizing power in 1789, they will take their revenge on those who have listened to them so little in the past before they relinquish, on sober second thought, the power the Internet will give them.

Part Two

LESSONS OF THE UNIMPEACHMENT — HOW THE FOURTH ESTATE BLEW IT

THE SEA CHANGE from the era of the Fourth Estate to the era of the Fifth was only partially impelled by the new possibilities the technology of the Internet offered to our citizens. Technological change combined with social change to transform the political landscape. As much as the Internet attracted us, the journalism and politics of the Fourth Estate have come to repel us. Over the almost thirty years between 1972 and 1999, the Fourth Estate alienated Americans even as the nation moved from stagnation to prosperity at home and from the Cold War to an era of American hegemony abroad. What happened? How did they blow it?

The debate during the unimpeachment of President Clinton offers a virtual CAT scan of our national political attitudes. A close examination of what went on and why it happened tells us all we need to know about the impatience of American voters with intermediaries of any description and our demand for direct control over our politics. In the events that shaped this ultimate political experience, we see the birth pangs of a new era of direct democracy struggling to be born.

Chapter Sixteen

HOW THE FOURTH ESTATE
TOOK POWER

SINCE THE BEGINNING of American politics, our system has been controlled by political bosses—dominating organizations and handpicking candidates at their will and whim. That era seems to be over. In the early nineteenth century, under the influence of his vice president, Martin Van Buren, Andrew Jackson initiated the era of party bosses.

Regardless of whether power lay with the Democrats or the Republicans, it was the party that controlled the government and the bosses that controlled the party. This uncontrollable symbiotic relationship endured for more than one hundred years and spawned legendary bosses such as Mayor Curley, Boss Tweed, Jim Farley, Ed Flynn, and Carmine DeSapio. It was only in the late 1950s that the bosses' widespread dominion was challenged. Eleanor Roosevelt helped initiate that process by speaking out

against the political bosses who controlled politics in New York
State. During the '60s the confrontation grew as citizens' grassroots, ad hoc organizations demanded a voice in the political process. Initially they expressed their views through civil rights, and
antiwar and citizens' movements, but their attentions quickly
turned to political action as the '60s unfolded.

On the conservative side of our political spectrum, ad hoc citizens' groups unexpectedly took power in 1964 when they forced
the Republican Party to nominate right-wing Senator Barry
Goldwater for president. The eastern Establishment bosses were
stunned by their loss of the party machinery to conservative constituency groups from southern and western states.

The Democratic bosses also began to lose their power in the
'60s as they stuck with President Lyndon Johnson even though
his Vietnam War policy was starting to alienate tens of millions of
Americans. Antiwar activists rallied behind the candidacy of
Senator Eugene McCarthy for president in 1968 and, after a
strong showing in the New Hampshire primary, forced Johnson
to drop out of the race for reelection. When Senator Robert
Kennedy announced his own candidacy, it seemed that the party
Establishment had finally lost control.

The bosses threw their support to Vice President Hubert
Humphrey, whose liberal credentials had been sullied by his support of the war. After Robert Kennedy's assassination on the
night he won the California primary, the bosses moved in boldly
to dictate Humphrey's nomination even though he had not won a

single primary. Antiwar activists responded angrily by demonstrating on the streets of Chicago outside the Democratic National Convention. While the whole world watched, Chicago Democratic chieftain Richard Daley ordered his police to put down the demonstration savagely and brutally while he jammed through Humphrey's nomination on the convention floor.

After these ham-handed tactics cost their party control of the White House in 1968, the Democratic Party bowed to voter demands and enacted far-reaching reforms that stripped power away from the legendary smoke-filled rooms of the bosses. Henceforth, in both parties, the vast majority of candidates came to be nominated directly through primary elections. For a while it seemed that American politics had finally heeded the message of the '60s and returned "power to the people."

But it proved to be a false dawn.

For the Democrats, procedural changes led to the disastrous McGovern campaign of 1972. The Nixon campaigns had already brought an anesthetizing force to grassroots Republicanism.

While the two parties were groping their way toward freedom from boss domination, a new force emerged—televised political advertising—that maintained the power of the elite. Just when that genuine participatory democracy was about to become a reality, the new political advertising effectively blocked such a new power shift.

The ascent of Richard Nixon to the White House in 1968 and his overwhelming reelection victory in 1972 were both products of a new, aggressive, and masterful use of paid television advertising to hypnotize the voters and lure them away from the grassroots forces newly beginning to assert themselves. The era of television began to settle in, tightening its grip on the political process and choking off grassroots politics like a superstore putting a neighborhood establishment out of business.

Aware of how advertising had blandly covered over the tactics that Nixon had used to win his 1972 reelection victory, the press struck back. Digging deeply, they uncovered a series of burglaries, dirty tricks, and shady deals that had smoothed the way toward Nixon's landslide win. Eventually the ultimate scandal emerged when it became clear that Nixon had used hush money to pay off Republican political operatives who had orchestrated the burglary of Democratic headquarters in the Watergate complex. As the president's efforts to use the FBI and CIA to cover his tracks became evident, he was forced from office.

In the aftermath of the Nixon saga, the two powers that animated the era of media domination—political advertising and investigative journalism—reigned supreme. Paid television advertising had elected a president. Aggressive and intrusive journalism had brought him down.

·   ·   ·

In 1998 the fire alarm of scandal sounded again. Once more, investigative journalists hounded a president's every move. In what seemed to be an eerie replay of Watergate, a special prosecutor closed in on a chief executive. Congress even voted impeachment for the first time since 1868. But the scandal fell flat. The public refused to answer the bell. A solid majority stayed firmly behind President Bill Clinton even as the evidence against him mounted.

The triumph of Bill Clinton over scandal was no isolated event. For more than a decade, the public had increasingly disregarded the media as it used scandal, its ultimate weapon, against politicians. When the media told us what to think, we refused to listen. They told us to reject Ronald Reagan as a lightweight, but we elected him president instead. Asked to drop him over the Iran-Contra scandal, we refused. We elected Clinton, reelected him, and stuck by him despite the daily pounding he took in the press. Bombarded by scandal from all sides, Clinton held on to our support and approval. Finally, when some asked us to remove him from office because he violated their idea of morality, we would not cooperate because he was meeting our needs.

· · ·

How did the media and the politicians blow it? Where has their power gone?

Chapter Seventeen

THE DECLINE OF
THE FOURTH ESTATE

PRESIDENT LYNDON B. JOHNSON used to keep three television sets in the Oval Office, one tuned to each of the big three networks—CBS, NBC, and ABC. That was it. That was the world. If it wasn't happening on one of those screens it wasn't happening. But the days of network monopolization of communications are long gone.

Why has the power and the prestige of the Fourth Estate fallen so low? Part of the reason is that Americans believe that the media is biased. In a May 20, 1999, survey of one thousand American voters, 47 percent said that the media was biased against Clinton while 23 percent felt it had a pro-Clinton orientation. Only 16 percent felt the media coverage of the unimpeachment was "largely free of any bias" and that the media had covered the impeachment fairly.

Ironically, each group felt that the media was biased against their point of view. Democrats, by fifty-eight to sixteen, felt that the media was against Clinton, while Republicans thought, by forty-two to thirty-two, that it was biased in his favor. The media couldn't do anything right.

Try as it might, the media could not interdict Clinton's relationship with the American people. Even before the unimpeachment, the American media fed voters a steady diet of scandal. During June 1996, for example, 32 percent of the minutes on the ABC, NBC, and CBS nightly news shows combined focused on the FBI file, Whitewater, Hillary's séance, or other Clinton controversies. During one memorable week in the middle of the month, each network news show was dominated by wall-to-wall coverage of scandal. Yet during the entire month, President Clinton's job-approval ratings and vote share against Dole dropped by only three points.

A large part of 1995 was devoted to Whitewater hearings by congressional committees. Hillary Clinton's appearances before the grand jury were accompanied by lurid headlines and detailed analyses of her legal predicaments. Yet, again, nothing happened. Three years later, in 1998, Whitewater accuser Senator Alfonse D'Amato lost his seat. The message: scandals don't work, and American voters distrust those who wallow in accusations.

Despite the best efforts of Washington's top investigative reporters Bob Woodward and Jeff Gerth, nobody seemed to care as accusation after accusation cascaded down on the public.

. . .

The media's constant obsession with scandal has cost it dearly in the opinions of most voters, particularly among Independents, the jump ball of our political process. As the media focused on digging up dirt, it lost its dignity and seemed, to most voters, to be pandering to our baser instincts in search of higher ratings. The media itself became the issue and people voted with their remote channel-clickers, changing the station and, finally, turning the set off and the computer on.

According to a Pew Research study in April of 1999, 38 percent of adults said that the news media was "immoral," compared with 13 percent who felt that way in 1985. A Harris poll in 1999 showed that the press ranked second-to-last in public confidence among twelve institutions, ahead only of labor unions. Only 14 percent expressed confidence in the press. Slightly more, 22 percent, had confidence in TV news, but institutions like the military, the Supreme Court, Wall Street, medicine, universities, religion, and big business outstripped TV news in public confidence.

But no matter how low the media has fallen in public esteem, voters would have no alternative but to put up with its bias had not technology offered an increasingly glittering array of other sources of information. The growth of cable news channels—Fox News Channel, CNN, MSNBC, CNBC, and C-SPAN—has breached the exclusive control of the flow of information that the press and networks once enjoyed. While the ratings of the network news shows of Dan Rather, Peter Jennings, and Tom Brokaw still dwarf the ratings of cable newscasters, the cumulative viewership of cable news stations clearly rivals that of the three nightly news shows.

But the Internet is causing even more significant erosion of the news monopoly of print and broadcast media. According to an April 1999 survey by Dresner, Wickers and Associates of one thousand Americans over the age of sixteen, "almost twenty-seven million people say they often read articles on news, sports, and other topics online." Dresner, Wickers estimates that twenty-two million use the Internet to read such articles just about every day, more than the number who watch any network anchor report the news on any given evening.

.   .   .

The trend is likely to continue. The Dresner, Wickers survey concludes that seventy-four million Americans use the Internet over the course of a two-month period. But the Net is addictive. Two-thirds of these Internet users—forty-five million people—report using it "pretty much every day."

The growth of the Internet is phenomenal. According to the Dresner, Wickers poll, one-quarter of the current Internet users have only begun to go online this year and another quarter started last year.

While the Internet has been moving up, the nightly news programs of the TV networks have been falling off in the ratings. Early in the decade, the three network evening news shows drew a combined total of 30 to 35 percent of all American households.

By 1995 their combined ratings had slipped to 23 percent. In August of 1999 they had fallen further, to a combined total of only 18 percent of American households.

People who surf the Net for their news have immediate access to wire-service stories directly from the Associated Press and need not concern themselves with what a newspaper editor will publish or a TV copyeditor can fit into a sound bite. They can and do browse, at their leisure, through the entire range of available news information. A simple comparison of the political news available on the Internet with that in even the best of daily newspapers shows how much more extensive is the range of stories offered on the Net. The following list compares the stories covered in the *New York Times* with those covered through America Online on a typical day.

These articles on national news were published in the *New York Times* on August 6, 1999:

- FCC Will Permit Owning Two Stations in Big TV Markets
- Some in GOP Join Democrats on HMO Bill
- SEC Fines a Bear Stearns Unit in Fraud Case after Long Inquiry
- Senate Confirms UN Appointment after 14 Months
- Tax Cut War Games
- Senators Say Errors Plagued U.S. Investigation of Possible Nuclear Spying by China

- Congressional Pact Alters Energy Department to Protect Nuclear Secrets
- Accord on Developing Land Beside the Grand Canyon

In addition to the above, the following articles on national news—*not* covered in the *Times* on August 6, 1999— appeared on AOL that day:

- Hatch Wants Probe of Clinton Judges
- States Seeing Worse Drought
- Deadline for Boeing 737 Repairs Met
- Afghan Arms Investigation Dropped
- Anthrax Vaccine Costs Pentagon
- More State Changes in Unwed Births

The TV news audience gets just one analysis, just one opinion, and just one editorial slant. The Net browser gets the news straight and multifaceted if he wants it—dozens and dozens of different views, thoughts, ideas, and opinions as he logs from Web site to Web site. No longer must he confine himself to what the local paper or the national and cable TV channels say. He can range far and wide, composing his own menu of favored outlets, columnists, and news sources. He gets the one thing the Fourth Estate cannot afford and still hope to keep its power: diverse information and diverse opinion.

·   ·   ·

Media influence is also declining because Americans are increasingly unwilling to trust opinion-makers whether inside or outside of the political process. More and more voters call themselves Independent and reject affiliation with either political party.

With greater levels of sophistication and education, people easily recognize manipulation in the media and come to discount a greater proportion of what they hear, read, and see. The ultimate Darwinian trait of our times, that which is most essential to our survival as a species, is the ability to spot propaganda or misleading information on television. Schooled to question ads and screen out the bulk of the information presented, Americans have become as expert as Russians once were in reading between the lines of the media to get at what is really going on.

Direct, primary sources of information resonate with voters far more than what they see on television or read in the press.

Bill Clinton came to realize that he could live without the media. Under constant attack in its pages and on its television programs, he came to rely on the kind of direct communication—through, around, under, and over the media—that will become normal during the era of the Fifth Estate. We wondered how he survived the negative press he got. It was by realizing, when others didn't, that the press mattered less and less.

Mike McCurry, Clinton's press secretary, was kept out of the inner councils of the administration. During the president's reelection campaign, McCurry was not invited to the weekly strategy meetings in the White House residence until late in the spring of 1996, after the meetings had been going on for a year and a half. White House spokesman during 1997–98, Lanny Davis, in his fair and balanced memoir, *Truth to Tell,* reports rarely even meeting with Clinton and admits that he was left to deal with third-string bureaucrats and lawyers. For Clinton the focus had become *his* sound bite, *his* paid advertising, *his* visuals—not the media filter through which they had to pass.

At the beginning, Clinton didn't realize that the power of the media was decreasing. In 1995 he returned from a speech before a youth group visiting the White House and recounted how he had explained American governance to the kids: "I couldn't tell them the truth, that the media runs the government, so I talked about the regular system of checks and balances they'd be more familiar with."

But the constant pounding Clinton took in the media didn't bring him down. Each week the president would be amazed that his poll ratings stayed high despite the never-ending negatives in the newspapers and on television. Eventually the president came to see the media through the perspective of its diminishing power and came to pay less attention to its barbs. Typically, in 1995 and 1996 Clinton did not read newspapers and barely skimmed each morning's stories from the nation's dozen top journals. He never watched TV news and rarely knew about negative stories. He paid attention to what he was saying and doing, confident that his message would get out regardless of what the media wanted.

Trying to scoop one another, members of the White House press corps fought for any scrap of news. But no matter how often ABC's Sam Donaldson or CNN's Wolf Blitzer hounded the president for answers, none were forthcoming. The media had lost the ability to use the threat of a public outcry to force Clinton to answer their questions. He could and did blithely ignore them without sustaining political damage.

The possibility of scandal forces politicians to give serious attention to the questions the media asks. In the past, politicians paid with their political lives if they dared disregard the press. When politicians didn't answer, withheld information, or lied to journalists, they would invite a firestorm of criticism. The articles and news segments would multiply until their cacophony became deafening. A wise political figure would sue for peace by full disclosure.

But those were the rules of the Fourth Estate. Clinton alone realized they had changed. The media had so lost its following that it could no longer force him to answer. He could answer questions at his leisure and dole out information as he chose. Nothing was as pathetic as the media's helplessness in the face of President Clinton's refusal to elaborate at his press conferences prior to the unimpeachment on what happened between him and Monica.

If the public won't get mad when politicians refuse to answer the media's questions, there is little a reporter can do to command an answer. The unimpeachment and the long succession of media-publicized scandals that have failed to make a dent in Clinton's approval ratings mark the halt in the growth of media power in America.

The Fourth Estate failed in 1999 to do what it had done in 1974—bring down a president. It lacked the audience, the credibility, and the prestige to succeed against Clinton as it had against Nixon.

Chapter Eighteen

THE DEATH OF SCANDAL

IN THE UNIMPEACHMENT, the press gave a scandal and nobody came. Voters refused to allow Clinton to be removed from office even though polls showed that the vast majority of Americans believed, in layman's language, that he had lied and covered up. Smaller numbers, but still a majority, even agreed that President Clinton had committed the crimes of perjury and obstruction of justice. But voters would not agree that his crimes deserved the punishment of removal from office.

Scandal-based politics requires a certain ceding of power from the voters to the inside players who investigate, unearth, publicize, and judge the wrongdoings of those whom we have elected to high public office. As we come to distrust the hunters more than the hunted, the dogs more than the fox, we jealously guard the right to decide during election times who should govern us.

We will not as easily be dissuaded from loyalty to those whom we have elected merely because of the incessant din of accusation and reproach that engulfs them. Even if the president has violated the law, we will not trust analysts to tell us whether or not he deserves to stay in office.

Some scandals concern issues that are abstruse to most voters. The complexities of the Iran-Contra affair required a detailed knowledge of American policy on hostages and of the Boland Amendment prohibiting aid to the Contras in Nicaragua. Both were well beyond the knowledge of the average American. The Whitewater scandal was similarly difficult for the typical voter to fathom. The intricacies of real estate deals and of bank regulation are not easily accessible to most people.

But everybody knows about sex, adultery, and extramarital affairs. There is nothing the experts know that the average person doesn't. It doesn't take a lawyer to understand what went on between Clinton and Lewinsky and why Clinton chose to lie about it. The idea of impeaching a president and removing him from office over lying about something personal and unofficial, and over a subject about which many American adults may have lied themselves, seemed preposterous to the average voter. Most people have neither taken nor paid a bribe to a public official. Most haven't abused power. But many have lied about sex at one time or another or could understand why someone else would do so.

Indeed, except for the most blatant and obvious examples of out-and-out financial corruption, scandal is weakened, if not actually dead, as a political force.

The most obvious reason for the lack of public outrage against exposé is its ubiquity. The controversies of the Clinton years have dulled us, leaving Americans jaded, complacent, and bored with the politics of accusation. As each day's newspapers and each night's television news carries with it somber warnings of a scandal that "raises serious questions," the voters have tuned out. They seem to be saying, in the words of Jack Germond's memoir of the 1984 presidential election, "Wake me when it's over."

The sheer magnitude of the Clinton scandals is dizzying— Gennifer Flowers; the draft; pot smoking; the nanny tax; gays in the military; the $200 haircut; the travel-office firings; the Foster suicide; the Espy, Brown, Cisneros, and Babbit investigations; Whitewater; the FBI files; the Rose Law Firm billing records; Chinese campaign contributions; advertising spending; Paula Jones; the China satellite waivers; the Web Hubbell job search; Chinese spies at Los Alamos. But Clinton has emerged with his ratings high. The public just stopped listening to stories about scandal.

Part of the responsibility lies with the partisanship in Washington. It is obvious to most voters that Republicans would be defending the conduct they now criticize and that Democrats would be attacking the behavior they now defend were the GOP to have won the 1992 and 1996 presidential elections. Scandal has become so obvious a partisan tool that voters have tended to discount a large part of what they hear. We seem to have lost our capacity to resolve such allegations. Few of the charges are ever adjudicated. There never seems to be a final determination of guilt or of innocence. The media just moves on to new accusations and innuendos.

Did Clinton do anything wrong in Whitewater? Did Hillary hide the billing records? Did the president know that the FBI files of prominent Republicans were being used illegally? Did he realize he was getting illegal Chinese campaign contributions? Who knows? Who will ever know? But Congress wouldn't remove Clinton because the voters wanted him to stay. He can't be indicted while in office. Likely Kenneth Starr won't go after him once Clinton's term is up. Even Starr's failure to prosecute does not clear the record since he will likely cite a lack of evidence rather than award Clinton a certificate of good health. So no question is ever really answered. Scandals involving the president don't end; as General Douglas MacArthur said of old soldiers, "they just fade away."

Scandal is also losing its clout because the subject matter has changed. No longer are scandals primarily about money or power, they have increasingly been about sex. Americans are becoming more like the French. Tour buses used to roll down the streets of Paris while the guides pointed out to gawking tourists where the mistress of President François Mitterand lived and where his out-of-wedlock children attended school. We could tour Versailles and see the quarters of Louis XIV's mistress. But in America all was puritan. Bill Clinton tested whether those limits still applied. They didn't. While Americans certainly do not approve of adultery by public officials, they are less willing to condemn people for private behavior.

. . .

But it wasn't just Clinton Luck that permitted his Houdini-like escape. Just as Clinton survived his scandal, so did Republican congressmen Henry Hyde (Illinois), Dan Burton (Indiana), Robert Barr (Georgia), and a number of others. Former House Speaker Newt Gingrich won reelection in 1994 despite charges that he had failed to pay child support. The resignation of Congressman Robert Livingstone (Louisiana) on the verge of his ascension to the House Speakership would appear to have been a voluntary resignation in the face of personal pain over a *potential* sex scandal, rather than a fall from public grace.

The lack of a national consensus on morals likely accounts for the declining probability that sexual indiscretions will destroy political careers. While some condemn homosexuality, adultery, or workplace sexual relationships, many others do not. Indeed, it would seem that voters actually apply lower expectations where sexual conduct is concerned. Had Clinton committed perjury about some paper bag loaded with hundred-dollar bills, rather than about adultery, one suspects he would be in early retirement today. If his obstruction of justice involved using the FBI or the CIA to haunt political opponents, as Nixon's did, then one cannot imagine that the public would be nearly as forgiving.

Throughout the unimpeachment, Clinton's defenders used the Internet wisely and well to project their argument that he should be left in office. Indeed, they pioneered the idea of Internet advocacy by establishing a new Web site, a precursor to

Vote.com called Moveon.com, that rallied sentiment against the congressional Republican obsession with Clinton's sex life. Hundreds of thousands of Clinton supporters logged on and used the site to make their support of the embattled president known.

The shrinking of the presidency as an institution has also contributed to the decline of scandal in our political life. Americans have stopped thinking of presidents as role models. Increasingly, we see the president in utilitarian terms. He's someone we can use to make our own lives better, a servant in the true sense of the word. As his personal conduct made it more and more impossible to look up to Clinton, voters were still able to approve of the job he was doing. He was no role model. Servants usually aren't. But he had his uses. With characteristic humility, Bill Clinton seemed to recognize the changes in the stature of the office he held. Knowing his personal failings, he seemed almost to downsize the job to a point where he could fill it well. We used to long for heroes to govern us. As members of the Fifth Estate we settle for human beings whether we like them or not.

George Washington couldn't tell a lie. Thomas Jefferson towered over his contemporaries as an intellect and a visionary. Abraham Lincoln's farseeing gaze from his monument throne in our capital sends chills down our spines. FDR's picture still hangs in the homes of many older Americans and JFK's often adorns the walls of their children's homes. One doubts that Bill Clinton's picture will ever make it out of our post offices.

The unimpeachment sharply split our views of Bill Clinton. No matter how harsh the charges became, more than 60 percent of us approved of his conduct on the job before, during, and after the unimpeachment. None of the seedy, seamy revelations did anything to dampen our positive outlook on his performance in office.

But as his job ratings remained high, his personal ratings crashed. Before the Lewinsky affair surfaced, 59 percent of Americans, according to one poll, rated Clinton favorably as a person. By the middle of March 1999, only 35 percent did so. As the following chart suggests, Clinton's personal ratings dropped week by week while his job approval remained high.

CLINTON'S JOB APPROVAL AND FAVORABILITY DURING THE UNIMPEACHMENT

Date	% Personal Favorability	% Job Approval
JANUARY 9, 1998	59	68
JANUARY 23	49	66
JANUARY 29	56	66
FEBRUARY 13	53	67
FEBRUARY 27	55	68
MARCH 27	55	68
APRIL 9	54	68
APRIL 24	54	68
MAY 8	50	67

Date	% Personal Favorability	% Job Approval
MAY 22	54	65
JUNE 5	53	66
JUNE 19	55	66
JULY 2	49	64
JULY 17	52	62
JULY 31	48	64
AUGUST 14	50	65
AUGUST 18	46	72
SEPTEMBER 11	44	68
SEPTEMBER 18	42	63
OCTOBER 9	42	65
OCTOBER 30	46	67
NOVEMBER 13	43	65
DECEMBER 4	41	69
DECEMBER 18	44	65
JANUARY 15, 1999	45	65
JANUARY 29	44	66
FEBRUARY 13	41	66
FEBRUARY 26	40	63
MARCH 12	35	65

(SOURCE: FOX NEWS/OPINION DYNAMICS POLL)

This incredible dichotomy between approval of his job performance and disapproval of our president as a person has never happened before. Usually the two benchmarks by which we measure our politicians move up or down in sync. For the first time, voters felt that it was okay to have a president of whom they did not approve personally.

This willingness to tolerate men or women of doubtful character in high office reflects how low "high" office has sunk in our esteem. The presidency has shrunk. No longer do we ask that it be reserved for heroes. A good day-to-day job is all we ask.

. . .

Personalities aside, the formal powers of the American presidency have become largely eroded. Although the president is commander in chief, he doesn't dare risk significant military casualties by using his power to send significant numbers of troops into combat. Only "safe" wars like Desert Storm or "air only" engagements like Kosovo are possible in our current political climate. The president's finger can still destroy us all by pushing the button, but, lacking an adversary, the danger seems remote.

Presidents can still appoint heads of executive branch agencies whose regulatory power is awesome, but congressional limits on their ability to bring havoc to our lives are increasingly reining them in. Deregulatory fervor hangs over Washington, forcing the FDA to be ever quicker in approving medicines, OSHA to be less intrusive, and the FAA to leave airlines alone. The president's power to regulate is clearly in remission.

Chief executives have the power to tax and spend with congressional approval, but getting that okay is no longer very easy. With Republicans in control of both houses of Congress, this president has had to learn to live with budget caps and spending limitations. The political corpses of former President George Bush and former Democratic House Speaker Tom Foley and Clinton's own loss of Congress in 1994 attest to how impossible it is to raise taxes in our current political landscape and survive.

But the most serious diminution in our presidency is the delegation of the president's power to run the economy to the chairman of the Federal Reserve Board. It is Alan Greenspan, not Bill Clinton, who runs the nation's financial and economic system. It is he, not the president, who decides how much unemployment or inflation to tolerate. The fundamental role of the American president—to keep the economy purring—has been delegated, Japanese-style, to a professional economist and skilled bureaucrat. It is the same system that generally has kept the Japanese economy strong through a succession of weak governments.

With the presidency thus shrunken, Clinton has turned his attention to small achievements that have traction in the lives of average Americans, the more specific and down-to-earth the better. As the presidency has come to be more about school standards, job training, welfare-to-work initiatives, and the potpourri of domestic politics, its grandeur has suffered. It is hard to imagine a president in top hat and tails, in the Versailles Hall of Mirrors, signing a document requiring a ratings system for sex and violence on television.

To replace the power to regulate the economy, the president has developed a new federal focus on education policy as the best way to raise personal incomes, particularly of those at the bottom of the scale. To replace the power to order troops into war, the president has focused on economic sanctions and air war to enforce his will, reserving his ground troops for peacekeeping missions. To replace his role as regulator, Clinton has used advocacy and public comment to promote decreased use of tobacco, warn of unsafe foods, and force greater responsiveness by TV networks to parental concerns.

While these steps are imaginative alternatives to the usual and more imperial powers of presidencies past, they do not inspire the same kind of awe that presidents once generated. With the decline in loftiness has come a more pragmatic view of the office and of its occupants. No longer are chief executives pseudomembers of our national family. Where Eisenhower may once have been our stand-in father, Kennedy our dashing husband, Johnson our eccentric old uncle, and Nixon the small-town banker next door, Bill Clinton is just our president. If we were to assign so familial a role to this chief executive, it would have to be as our philandering adolescent son—hardly an image calculated to enhance the stature of the office he holds.

Clinton stimulated this diminishment in our nation's expectations when he campaigned in 1992 as everyman, riding the bus with the Gores and jogging in his baggy shorts, pausing to lunch at McDonald's. His efforts to bring a dignity to his stature by ministering to the nation in the aftermath of the Oklahoma City bombing and preaching parental responsibility never fully replaced everyman in the nation's impression of its forty-second president.

Early in 1995, he would often speak of something he had to do, some speech he must give, or a ceremony at which he was expected to preside, as "something I have to do because I'm president." His almost apologetic diminishment of the grandeur of his office might well have related to an inner sense that he could never live up to the moral and personal standards of his predecessors. He knows himself well enough to bring the job down to his level.

Some have derided the president's focus on small steps and specific achievements and have said that he is reducing the prestige of the presidency to the level of a governor. The more accurate metaphor would be a mayor.

People need the things a mayor does in very concrete ways. They need to have their garbage collected, their streets policed, their homes protected from fire, and their schools kept open and safe. But in times of prosperity and peace, few voters really need a president. Most have their financial lives set and can afford to look at the presidency as an abstraction in a way they could never contemplate their local mayor. But Clinton has changed that by injecting his administration into the nitty-gritty of everyday life. Do you need guns taken off your street? He passed the Brady Bill. Worried about the quality of your schools? He's increased education funding. Concerned about sending your child to college? He's raising scholarship aid.

While we might like to see a role model for our children in our national chief executive, nobody really has the same expectations of their mayor. Few New York City babies are going to be named

"Rudy" in honor of Mayor Giuliani. It doesn't happen that way. If the mayor does a reasonably good job of picking up our trash, policing our streets, and running our schools, we don't much care whether or not he sets a good example. His private life is his own business and all we ask is that he does a good job of serving us.

·   ·   ·

Most modern presidents have suffered from episodic scandals of some kind. Truman's second term was almost destroyed by one scandal after another. It is only in recent times that historical alchemy has transformed his corruption-plagued administration into one of the "near-great" presidencies. Eisenhower's administration was marred by the forced resignation of his chief of staff, Sherman Adams, amid the president's pathetic plea, "I need him." Walter Jenkins's sex scandal and Abe Fortas's financial misdeeds plagued the Johnson years.

Scandal reached its true apogee in the '70s. Amid Vietnam, Watergate, and the energy crisis, voters held politicians in particularly low regard. Mere accusation was enough to destroy the careers of many able public servants. Negative ads savaged incumbents and single-issue politics controlled the electoral process. Willing to see evil in any set of even vaguely suspicious facts, voters saw every campaign contribution as a bribe, every foreign trip as a junket, and every missed vote as damning evidence of dereliction of duty.

In this environment, allegations of scandal flourished. So intense was the suspicion that even a model of rectitude like

President Jimmy Carter had to ask his attorney general to appoint a special prosecutor to investigate the agricultural subsidies on his peanut farm to prove that he had not done anything wrong. Reagan Labor Secretary Raymond Donovan had to resign amid accusations of malfeasance. When he was acquitted years and years later, he asked memorably, "Where do I go to get my reputation back?" Unsuccessful presidential candidate Gary Hart fell victim to his affair with Donna Rice, while President Clinton was able to survive similar allegations four years later.

During the '80s, public attitudes toward scandal changed. No longer were accusations coming at leaders we didn't really like—Johnson, Nixon, or Carter—but now a man we adored, Ronald Reagan, was also being put through the mill. More and more, we learned to look past scandals and even to keep our high esteem intact for many at whom charges were leveled. We began to call Ronald Reagan the "Teflon president" because accusations of misconduct or neglect of his job just washed off him. Did he fall asleep in meetings? Was he beholden to special interests? Were his budget cuts too harsh? Was the Pentagon awash in procurement scandals? Did the budget deficit triple? Had he tried to freeze cost-of-living adjustments on Social Security? It didn't make any difference. Americans stood by Ronald Reagan because they felt they knew him and they distrusted his accusers more.

It was the Iran-Contra affair, which surfaced right after the 1986 elections, that showed the fundamental change in our attitudes. Surveys all showed that we thought Reagan was lying. We refused to believe him when he said he knew nothing about the swap of arms to Iran in return for the release of hostages and claimed he did not realize that the Saudis were funneling weapons to the Contras in Nicaragua. But we didn't particularly care. After all, voters reasoned, Reagan acted from the best of motives—wanting to free the hostages to return them to their families—and the Contras were fighting the good fight against communism in Central America. His popularity remained high and his job approval sank only gradually and slightly. In a political equivalent of jury nullification in a criminal trial, voters rendered a split verdict in the case of scandal: guilty but not deserving of punishment.

At the same time, voters became more skeptical of negative advertisements. Most political consultants came to realize that the pendulum had begun to shift against negatives and for rebuttal advertising. Annoyed by Bush's use of racial symbol Willie Horton to attack Democratic nominee Mike Dukakis in 1988 as soft on crime, voters began to turn off negative ads for the same reasons that they were coming to discount accusations.

Then came Bill Clinton. Attacked with negative ads on the one hand and newspaper allegations of corruption, indiscretion, and malfeasance on the other, he seemed to walk through unscathed. As his administration unfolded, voters came to expect that news coverage of the Clinton administration would be replete with allegations of all sorts, but the press had cried wolf too often for most to care. Despite the daily shower of revelations, his job approval remained high.

Clinton's confidence in the face of scandal was a long time in coming. At first he felt as vulnerable to political embarrassment as any modern politician does. "You can't tell me this drip, drip, drip, drip isn't having an effect!" Clinton screamed, red-faced, at the July 3, 1996, weekly session on White House campaign strategy. "Every innocent person they drag through the mud, every honest mistake they call a shocking scandal, every item of information they twist out of all proportion—you can't tell me that's not killing me out there."

But as the accusations passed by and his ratings remained high, his confidence grew. He won reelection handily despite exhaustive coverage of the FBI-file scandal five months before the election and of the campaign-contributions imbroglio in the two weeks before balloting began. By the unimpeachment of 1998–99, Clinton realized that he didn't have to give an inch in the face of accusations. He could stonewall and he would win. Scandal was indeed losing its ability to destroy political careers. It was losing its punch.

As a result of this pleasant discovery, the president felt free to ignore blatantly reporters' questions and to refuse overtly to discuss the Lewinsky affair at his press conferences. He became politically free to ignore the inquiries, sending maddeningly evasive answers to the House Judiciary Committee's interrogatories— precipitating, in the opinion of many, his own impeachment. Was he unwise to do so? In the end, he retained the right to serve out his term. Every last day of it.

As the '90s progressed and scandals seemed to bounce off Clinton like bullets off Superman, voters were demanding much greater proof before they would believe accusations of misconduct. While Americans were once quick to leap to verdicts of guilt based on press accounts, they are now showing a reluctance to believe the accuser.

Was he making his charges in return for money? Was the accuser an inveterate scandalmonger? Did he have an axe to grind? Was excessive partisanship involved? The burden of proof on accusers became greater than ever before. He who asserted had better be ready to prove, and to undergo a gauntlet of criticism while he's at it.

Yet proof is very hard to come by without subpoena power and, as the Republicans have found out, not easy to uncover even with it. The din of outrage that accompanies the public exposure of public figures is simply not heard much beyond the beltway that surrounds Washington, D.C.

Procedural offenses no longer send the public into a feeding frenzy, as much as they continue to annoy the press and opposition politicians. The administration that is lax in complying with subpoenas need not fear a massive public backlash. The frequency of the subpoenas that rained down on the Clinton White House from Congress has undermined the importance of each subsequent summons.

Many have focused on the United States Supreme Court's decision in the Paula Jones case to permit a president to be sued civilly while he is still in office. In their hilarious opinion, the justices said that they felt that permitting such suits would not constitute an "undue burden" on the presidency. Like hell it didn't!

But of equal importance is Kenneth Starr's implied opinion that a president cannot be prosecuted *criminally* while he is still in office. If this precedent holds, there is no real forum, short of impeachment, in which the guilt or innocence of an accused president can be determined. Since nobody seems eager to undertake another impeachment anytime soon, one is tempted to ask "scandal, where is thy sting?" If the public requires proof in order to be outraged and the judicial process prohibits a criminal trial of a president, which is the only way to get the proof, scandal has no place to go. It's a dead-end street.

There will still be scandals. There will still be politicians led off to jail in handcuffs. But the daily diet of scandal, on which the press has gorged the American people since 1992, has run its course—not because the press will stop writing, but because the public will stop caring. Without scandal as a theme, the Fourth Estate has no means by which to exert control over the political process.

In the void created by the death of scandal, members of the Fifth Estate will be able to focus on what is truly important in the national agenda.

Chapter Nineteen

DIRECT COMMUNICATION
WINS OUT

PRESIDENTS' DAY IS in February, but January, when the president gives the State of the Union address, is the president's month. More than any other presidency, the Clinton administration has come to be defined in terms of these annual speeches. These addresses, which have always given presidents a short-term lift, have proven to be the seminal events of his tenure in office. Every year, the impact of the density and substance of Clinton's presentations, and of his skill at elucidating his program before the country, lasts long after he has left the rostrum and the applause has faded. Despite frequent media complaints that his speeches are too long, detailed, boring, and political, voters have tuned in, paid attention, and remembered what he said for months afterward. The instant analysis of pundits and experts has mattered little.

There is no better example of the growth of direct democracy than the Clinton State of the Union addresses. These have not been one-shot or episodic peaks as they were in previous administrations. The ideas and proposals he presents in these addresses act like the cables of a suspension bridge, holding the entire span aloft in the months that follow. As the effect of his eloquence slowly wears off, his ratings dip like those cables of the bridge, only to recover during the next address. These annual speeches are the buttresses of his presidency. Without them the entire structure would fall. It is the heights he reaches at the end of every January that enable his administration to remain popular.

In the nineteenth century, before the invention of the microphone, politicians required a good set of lungs in order to be heard by an audience. Today it takes a president who is good at presenting his program in these annual addresses. Clinton's skill in these expositions of his views is truly the defining factor in making his presidency work.

So complete is his mastery of the forum that, in 1994 when his TelePrompTer operator fed the wrong speech to him for the first fifteen minutes of his address, Clinton, unfazed, gave the speech from memory while the aide struggled to get the right text onto his machine. When it finally came, the president switched from his memory to the prompter text without a slip. Nobody in the live or television audience realized that he had been giving the speech, word for word, from memory for fifteen minutes—about thirty pages of text!

Why were these annual speeches so valuable to his political health?

Earlier in the age of television, presidents addressed the nation far more frequently than they do today. Now the television networks, hungry for advertising revenue, refuse to cancel their prime-time programming for a presidential address unless the sky is falling. During all of 1995 and 1996, President Clinton addressed the nation only twice over television, apart from his State of the Union address and his Democratic Convention acceptance speech. In mid-1995 he spoke to announce his balanced-budget proposal and then he spoke again later in the year to justify the dispatch of twenty-five thousand American troops to Bosnia. Each address lasted ten minutes or less.

The networks were grudging about allowing the balanced-budget speech and it took a series of personal phone calls from Vice President Gore to get them to accept. His rationale—that the nation would face a government shutdown and needed to be told to prepare for it—was somewhat weak, and Presidential Press Secretary Mike McCurry privately related that the network executives were angered and felt manipulated and abused in granting the time for the speech. By contrast, Presidents Kennedy, Johnson, and Nixon were able to address the nation as they pleased and made frequent use of the opportunities to build support for their policies.

In the absence of other public forums, the State of the Union speech has become a completely unique event for the president.

At no other time can a president spend a full hour, on all networks and cable news stations, laying out and explaining his program to an audience that includes a majority of the likely general-election voters. Unhurried, he can explain what he wants to do and why he wants to do it. He can address the nation from the most dignified of podiums, without interruption and without press spin, until his address has run its full course.

Clinton has always badly needed the lift he gets from his State of the Union speeches, but never more so than in 1995 as he reeled from massive defeat in the congressional elections of 1994. Entering the election with handsome majorities in both the House and the Senate, he performed a feat unequaled since Harry Truman in 1950—losing both houses of Congress. As Clinton entered the House chamber to begin his remarks, the doorkeeper intoned, solemn as always, "Mr. Speaker, the President of the United States." Members applauded, some even cheered, but the procession to the rostrum had a distinctly funereal aspect to it.

Clinton began his speech by accepting the results of the election and calling on the Republicans to work with him on America's needs: "We must agree that the American people voted for change. . . . Now all of us, Republicans and Democrats alike, must say, 'We hear you. We will work together to earn the jobs you have given us.'"

Crafting a centrist course, he appealed for protection of Medicare from the Republican budget axe, foreshadowing the themes that would bring him back to political power as the year unfolded.

The speech dragged on for more than an hour. Media pundits ridiculed Clinton for his filibuster and joked that most of America fell asleep. The Fourth Estate underestimated the appeal the long speech would have among the general public. Soon all had to eat their words as polls showed that the speech had breathed life into his nearly cold political corpse.

Americans had come to appreciate depth and detail in political communications. The Establishment media, forced to condense its offerings to short sound bites, had come to assume that people could not pay attention for more than a few minutes at a time. They wrongly believed that the long, detailed specificity of the speech would put the electorate to sleep. They were wrong. The same force that impelled viewers to watch all-news television channels for hour after hour, or to surf the Net reading everything they could find, kept them glued to the screen as Clinton rambled on, spelling out his agenda for America.

The 1996 State of the Union speech was written in happier circumstances. Having decisively defeated the Republicans in the government shutdowns of November and December of 1995, Clinton had gained a narrow lead in the polls against his GOP challenger, Bob Dole. By the time he sat down after another one-hour speech, his lead over Dole had soared to seventeen points. It stayed there until the election, only dropping to eight points just before election day.

The speeches Clinton gave in 1998 and 1999 were the most important elements in his survival of the attempt to remove him from office. By a curious coincidence, the Lewinsky affair was first unmasked in public on January 21, 1998, only six days before the president gave his address. His 1999 speech came right in the middle of the Senate trial. He gave the speech the day after the House prosecutors had finished presenting their devastating three-day case to America and to the senators who were sitting as jury. At his hour of maximum peril, the president had his strongest weapon at hand—the State of the Union speech.

When Clinton entered the House chamber in January of 1998, calls for his resignation had been filling the air, ever since his affair with Lewinsky had been revealed. Serious political observers wondered if he could weather the storm. By his flat declaration the day before he spoke to the Congress, that "I did not have sex with that woman . . . Monica Lewinsky," he managed to still the clamor for his head, but his popularity sagged to new depths. Undaunted, Clinton gave a memorable speech focusing on his ability to balance the budget. He insisted that none of the budget surplus should be tapped until a viable program to save Social Security was in place. His performance won its usual positive response from the public and his poll numbers recovered. It seemed that he would, indeed, live to fight again another day.

His next State of the Union speech literally saved his presidency. Coming after the House of Representatives had voted articles of impeachment for the first time since 1868, Clinton's situation was desperate. The days immediately before the speech had not been kind to the forty-second president. House managers had appeared day after day on television, laying out in precise and chilling detail their evidence that the president had committed perjury and obstructed justice. So convinced was the nation, that more than 60 percent felt that Clinton had lied before the grand jury and more than 50 percent felt that he had obstructed justice.

On the day of his speech his attorneys presented a technical, legalistic defense that pivoted around the ridiculous proposition that the word "sex" did not include oral sex and that the president had not obstructed justice when he carefully coached his secretary, Betty Currie, to deny that he had ever been alone with Monica Lewinsky. Clinton's 1999 State of the Union address had to be a tour de force. And it was. Aiming his proposals and arguments at Senate Democrats who held his acquittal majority in their hands and at Generation X voters who were essential to his popular majority, he struck all the right notes and themes. His proposals covered the gamut of public concerns and had something for everybody.

Proposals in Clinton's 1999 State of the Union Speech:
For workers:
   • Raising the minimum wage
For parents:
   • Hiring 100,000 new teachers to cut class sizes
   • Aid for school construction and renovation
   • Fighting teen smoking

For patients:

- A bill of rights for managed health care

For the elderly:

- Medicare for those over fifty-five

For working mothers:

- More child care

For the environment:

- Clean-water initiative

- Combating global warming

For business:

- Fast Track trade legislation

The results of the speech were swift and sure. The momentum of the prosecution stalled and Senate Democrats stuck firmly by their president.

In broader terms, the effectiveness of State of the Union speeches shows the enormous impact of direct communication with voters, unfiltered by the press prism that normally filters all of a political leader's messages. This opportunity for a president to speak directly, at length and in detail about his programs, transcends the daily press noise and decisively molds the political dialogue for months to come.

In recent years voters have paid less and less attention to the daily reports of the Fourth Estate. President Clinton's ratings were largely unaffected by his media coverage. The electorate of the new Fifth Estate tunes in when the president speaks directly.

Patiently they watch his speech and, at its conclusion, retain his message for months and months to come. The superiority of the attention paid to this once-a-year, one-hour speech, compared with that paid to the daily hour-upon-hour of press coverage, attests vividly to the waning power of the Fourth Estate and the growing clout of direct communication.

C-SPAN has become the average politician's vehicle for direct communication. During 1996 Clinton's polls showed that 20 percent of the voters indicated that they had watched C-SPAN during the preceding thirty days. When one in five voters watches a speech directly, often putting up with a boring delivery and a seemingly endless text, it shows the demand for raw information, unfiltered by press interpretation, that predominates as the Fifth Estate takes over.

No one has been more conscious of the power of his annual speeches than Clinton himself. For months before the speech, the White House staff canvasses federal agencies, friends of the president, and think tanks for ideas that need to be mentioned. The president's own active imagination contributes mightily to the search. Indeed, the rhythms of the executive branch are distinctly built around the State of the Union speech. It became the basic planning document of the Clinton White House.

In 1999 Republicans were baffled when the momentum they had built with their prosecution statements before the Senate dissipated as the president addressed the nation. But Clinton knew all along that he would never be removed from office. At least not in January.

Chapter Twenty

HOW THE POLITICIANS
BLEW IT — PARTISANSHIP MADE
AMERICANS SICK

IN WASHINGTON the partisan divide yawns wide. In the rest of America, party conflict used to elicit only wide yawns. Now it brings a sneer.

In the era of the Fourth Estate we tolerated partisanship. It seemed the inevitable accompaniment to democracy and politics. But as interparty warfare has become more rancorous and has infected everything in Washington, voters in the emerging era of the Fifth Estate are losing patience with it. Partisanship is the single biggest disconnect between the American people and their government.

In Washington, this verse from Gilbert and Sullivan's operetta *Iolanthe* would be applicable:

> Nature always doth contrive
> That every boy and every gal

Who's born into the world alive

Is either a little li-ber-el

Or else a little conserrrr-vitive

But in the world beyond the District of Columbia beltway, party loyalties are fading fast. Soon a majority of Americans will profess no party allegiance, while all of Washington is sure to remain strictly divided along party lines for decades, if not centuries, to come.

The Independent voters who dominate the American electorate simply do not invest in the assumptions that loyal Democrats and loyal Republicans share. They see no constructive reason why a president of one party should meet with almost reflexive opposition from members of the other party. To them, each decision should be taken on its own merits. The Washington assumption that government is a game in which two teams oppose each other is just not shared by the American voters.

The physical layout of the chambers of Congress, in a semicircle, is far more reflective of the views of the average person than is the face-to-face configuration of the Labor and Conservative benches in England's House of Commons. To the average American Independent voter, the conflicts between Democrats and Republicans most resemble the circular, revenge-seeking, mindless feuding of the Capulets and the Montagues in Shakespeare's *Romeo and Juliet.*

As long as the partisanship of Washington was limited and tempered, Americans tolerated it. But now that it has grown to

encompass every issue, every procedure, and almost every confirmation vote, they are losing their patience. While citizens once
treated party confrontation indulgently as something politicians
do that can't be avoided, now they see it as a real obstacle to
meeting their needs. As Washington becomes more partisan and
less civil, voters won't put up with it. To most people, the unimpeachment was the high-water mark of partisanship.

. . .

Ironically, as the ideological differences between the parties seem
to fade and their joint success at creating a pretty good country
grows, their mutual animosity escalates. Recent decades have
seen an almost total erosion of civility and consensus among
Washington's political leaders. In the '50s and '60s, partisanship
was normally subordinated to decorum and deference. Gradually
the boundaries expanded; more of what was traditionally above
party became caught in the crossfire of political combat.

Supreme Court nominations, for example, were relatively
uncontroversial throughout our history. It was not until the
Republicans forced Johnson appointee Abe Fortas from the high
court bench in the 1960s that appointments to the court were
mired in controversy. Enraged Democrats retaliated by blocking
the confirmation of Nixon Supreme Court appointees Hainsworth
and Carswell and Reagan's nomination of Robert Bork. While
Clarence Thomas was confirmed, his approval was held up for
months by allegations of sexual harassment. Increasingly, a nominee's ability to get confirmed is a major factor in a president's

decision to appoint him to the high court. As a direct result, the court has drifted to the center since nominees of the left and the right usually muster a majority in the reflexively partisan Senate. The Supreme Court nomination process, once a presidential prerogative subject to only routine and minimal legislative scrutiny, has now become a national theater for venting political passion.

Cabinet positions, once routinely approved by the Senate, have also become frequent forums for partisan clashes. At the start of his administration, President Bush suffered the defeat of his nomination of former Senator John Tower of Texas as defense secretary, while Clinton's choice, at the start of his second term, of Tony Lake to head the CIA ran into lethal and largely partisan opposition.

Sometimes the motivation for opposing a presidential cabinet nominee is to embarrass the administration, particularly early on as it seeks to gain momentum. Clinton's inability to nominate an attorney general who could get confirmed in the opening months of his first term gave the public an impression that he couldn't get his act together and wasn't up to the job.

Often the opposition to a nominee is a surrogate way to litigate public policy, as when the GOP refused to confirm Clinton's appointment of Dr. Henry W. Foster as surgeon general because he had performed a handful of abortions during his medical career. Similarly, Clinton's choice of Lani Guinier as assistant attorney general for civil rights in his first term served the GOP as an ideal opportunity to attack racial quotas and affirmative action.

Like the Israeli-Palestinian conflict or the Albanian-Serbian cycle of vengeance, where each act of violence kindled the outrage to fuel the next one in an endless circle of retaliation, partisanship spread throughout the '70s, '80s, and '90s to each facet of political life.

The filibuster, once reserved for extreme situations, has become the norm in the Senate. Back in the '50s the southern senators would threaten to use the rule permitting limitless floor debate to kill civil rights legislation. The threat of a filibuster usually sufficed to force a compromise. Only rarely did the southern bloc of senators actually take to their feet and try to talk a bill to death, but the threat was always there.

Throughout the years of the civil rights struggle, liberals railed against the filibuster, calling it a restraint on democracy. They attacked the ability of a willful minority to frustrate the national consensus and they fought to lower the number of votes needed to shut off debate (called closure) when Senate rules were adopted at the start of each new Congress. First Hubert Humphrey and his band of merry liberals succeeded in reducing the requirement for closure from two-thirds of the Senate to two-thirds of those present and voting. Then in the '60s they cut the closure requirement to sixty votes. The filibuster did not become routinely used until the Republicans took control of both the White House and the Senate, from 1981 until 1986. Then the outnumbered Senate Democrats began to filibuster frequently. By the '80s and '90s the filibuster had come out of disrepute and was seen by both parties—and by liberals and conservatives—as a standard weapon in their partisan wars.

During the first two years of the Clinton presidency, when Democrats controlled both Congress and the White House, the GOP made the filibuster a daily event. So common was its use that only rarely did the Republicans actually have to stand in the well of the Senate and hold the floor for weeks on end. By the time the Republicans took back control of Congress in 1994, the filibuster was standard operating procedure. No longer did it take fifty-one votes to pass a law in the Senate. It now took sixty. If Senate majority leader Bob Dole (R-Kansas) couldn't get the sixty votes he needed to shut off debate under the Senate rules, he just didn't bother to bring the bill up for a vote.

The tide of partisan aggression in Washington rose to a new level in 1995 when the Republicans who controlled Congress let the government shut down rather than give way on their draconian budget cuts. Claiming inaccurately that only with their dramatic cuts in spending could the budget come into balance, they refused to compromise and defeated interim funding to keep federal agencies open when the fiscal year ended. In late November of 1995, and again during Christmas, all routine business of the federal government came to a halt. Like some third-world country in the midst of a coup, government bureaus shuttered their doors, the White House staff had to stay home, and the president's office was manned by volunteers. (This situation is what elevated Monica Lewinsky to a new station in the chief of staff's office, filling in for regular employees. It was there that Clinton met her.) By the time the GOP regained its senses and reopened the government, Republicans had suffered badly and destroyed public confidence in their leadership.

Against this backdrop of rising partisanship and increasing confrontation, the unimpeachment was the last straw. Americans had a hard time seeing the unimpeachment as anything other than the next step in the inexorable increase in the venom and intensity of party warfare in our nation's capital. Having subjected one after another of the routine operations of government to partisan combat, it was only natural that one day somebody would try to oust a duly elected president. It was the logical next step.

But likely it will be the last.

Most voters felt that were a Republican president to be guilty of the same offenses as was Bill Clinton, his accusers would become the GOP president's defenders and Democrats would become the prosecutors. To the lawyers who make up more than half of the Congress, this role-playing and advocacy seems normal and even desirable. For them the adversary system is the best way to arrive at the truth. But for the average American, equally distrustful of lawyers and of politicians, it sounds like the height of hypocrisy.

Ever since the failure of their efforts to shut down the government, mainstream Republicans have understood how their partisanship had rubbed voters the wrong way. Anxious to play down their reputation for visceral party combat, they have been anxious to compromise with the Democrats. House Speaker

Dennis Hastert (R-Illinois) has called for a lowering of voices, and congressmen from both parties traveled to a special conference in Hershey, Pennsylvania, to sample the chocolate and discuss ways to bring civility back to the congressional dialogue.

But during the unimpeachment the firebrands on the right in the House of Representatives showed that they didn't get the message. To the embarrassment of their elders in the Senate, they pushed forward recklessly with their effort to remove an elected president from office using the ultimate sanction of impeachment. Like the charge of the Light Brigade during the Crimean War, immortalized in Tennyson's poem, they rode "into the valley of death, into the mouth of hell . . . as cannon in front of them volleyed and thundered." As with the Light Brigade, they were destroyed. And, as after that heroic charge, warfare changed. So the unimpeachment is likely to bring about a reversal of decades of escalating party warfare.

Public impatience with partisan conflict stems from the fact that most voters do not support either political party. Disliking both parties equally, the 40 percent of American voters who profess to be Independents regard party warfare with the same lack of interest that those who don't follow baseball have about watching a game on television. As tedious pitch follows tedious pitch and inning follows inning, they become bored, restless, and eventually angry at having to watch. Seeing Democrats and Republicans tear at each other in the unimpeachment was like being forced to watch a game that runs deep into extra innings. While the nation's problems piled up on the Senate's doorstep, each day was devoted to the worst spectacle of partisan wrangling in decades. America has finally had enough. As Independents, most voters are driven to distraction by party conflict. They just don't have a dog in that fight.

Most Americans would now heartily agree with the Father of Our Country, George Washington, in his harsh condemnation of political parties:

> ". . . all combinations and associations . . . with the real design to direct, control, counteract, or awe the regular deliberation and action of the constituted authorities, are destructive . . . and of fatal tendency. They serve to organize faction, to give it an artificial and extraordinary force; to put in the place of the designated will of the nation, the will of a party, often a small but artful and enterprising minority of the community. . . ."

At first Clinton embraced partisanship and made it his style of governance. Determined to use his majorities in the House and the Senate to pass his programs, he pursued doggedly his party's agenda of healthcare reform, abortion liberalization, gun control, and raising taxes on the wealthy while expanding subsidies to the working poor.

When the voters dealt him a Republican-dominated Congress in the election of 1994, Clinton briefly dallied with bipartisanship but soon reverted to his old habits, castigating the GOP for cutting school lunches and warning that they wanted to send children to orphanages.

But by mid-1995 Clinton came to realize how disgusted voters were with party dogmatism. He began to reach across party lines to embrace Republican objectives of a balanced budget and welfare reform. As the Republicans shut down the government because they could not get their harsh cuts enacted, Clinton was able to position himself above the battle and above party—in a way that George Washington would have loved.

When the GOP's anger and fervor led to the impeachment, Clinton was able to paint their efforts as partisan and mean-spirited. Despite his tawdry personal behavior, Clinton seemed to rise in stature as the Republicans appeared to wallow in bitterness, reproach, and self-interest. Clinton had learned how to play the game of bipartisanship to slip a punch.

The increasing disrepute in which parties are held further opens the way for the Fifth Estate. People no longer need party functionaries to tell them what to think and how to act. Party leaders are anachronistic in the age of the Internet. As the voter turns against parties, he turns toward direct expression of his opinions on the Net, sometimes siding with one party and sometimes with the other. To members of the Fifth Estate, parties will become even weaker than they are today.

Chapter Twenty-one

CONGRESS IS LOSING ITS POWER

THE PRESIDENCY HAS lost stature as the power of the Fifth Estate emerges. Congress has lost even more.

The past decade has seen a major shift in the epicenter of power from the legislative to the executive branches of our government. During both the 1995–96 government shutdowns and the unimpeachment, Bill Clinton showed how the executive branch was superior to the legislative in a dogfight. This presidency is a Fifth Estate institution.

Congress is mired in the mind-set of the Fourth Estate. It is losing the respect of the American people, and blowing its credibility and its prestige more and more with each passing year. Even as the presidency shrinks by focusing on more mundane problems and losing some of its imperial stature, Congress loses even more power. Government is getting smaller. But it's the president's government. Not Congress's.

From the inception of our Republic, the executive and legislative branches have struggled for dominance. The checks and balances built into our Constitution make the conflict inevitable.

In the Constitution the legislative power is supreme. Article I deals with the powers of Congress. The executive branch has to wait for Article II. But in the early years of the Republic, the stature of presidents like Washington, Jefferson, and Jackson gave the executive the upper hand. As the Civil War approached and our presidents were nonentities like Franklin Pierce and James Buchanan, the center of power shifted to Congress, where men like Daniel Webster, Henry Clay, and John C. Calhoun set the political agenda.

Lincoln used his wartime powers and his superb skills as a communicator to concentrate power in the presidency again, but the impeachment of his successor, Andrew Johnson, helped to shift power back to Congress. The corruption of some presidents and the ineptitude of others kept the executive subservient to the legislative for the balance of the nineteenth century.

Activist, internationalist presidents Theodore Roosevelt and Woodrow Wilson returned dominance to the presidency until the Johnson era. With strong chief executives like FDR, Truman, Kennedy, and Johnson, the center of political action was in the White House, not in Congress.

With Nixon's ouster, the momentum shifted back to the Congress as it cut the powers of the president. The War Powers

Act, passed over a presidential veto, limited the commander in chief's ability to commit troops without congressional approval. Senator Frank Church's investigation curbed the power of the executive branch intelligence agencies. In its most serious bid for power, the legislative branch created the Congressional Budget Office so Congress could meet the administration on equal terms in developing budgets and spending priorities.

Early in his administration, President Reagan took back some executive authority by skillfully using the new budgetary procedures to impose his program of tax cuts, defense increases, and social spending cuts on a Democratic House of Representatives. The resulting huge increase in the budget deficit strait-jacketed both Congress and the president and forced a fiscal discipline on both branches of government that stripped them of much of their ability to legislate and spend.

By the time Bush and Clinton came to power, the conflict between the branches was in full swing. With Congress controlled by one party and the White House by another for all but two years of the Bush and Clinton presidencies, the battle between the institutions at opposite ends of Pennsylvania Avenue became a national struggle for power.

In 1995 Congress sought to dominate the White House by taking the initiative in slashing government spending and passing Newt Gingrich's Contract with America. The war between the branches escalated to a level almost unique in our history. Congress used the budget-making authority it had voted itself in the '70s and '80s to force a program of spending cuts down the throat of the president. With strict discipline, the GOP passed its budget and balked at serious negotiations with the White House. Since Senate rules precluded a filibuster on a budget resolution, the Democratic minority could only watch in frustration and rage as the Republicans jammed their budget through and dared Clinton to veto it.

On the surface of this confrontation lay an ideological struggle for control of the government. Underneath, however, lay an institutional bid for power by a rebellious and arrogant Congress that summoned memories of the bid of radical Republicans like Thaddeus Stevens and Ben Wade for domination in the years after Lincoln died.

At the height of the virtual civil war between the Democratic president and the Republican Congress, the GOP presented Clinton with its budget and said, in effect, take it or leave it. When Clinton vetoed the budget, the GOP refused to let the government operate. As the battle escalated between Clinton and Congress, the president's advantage in a war of words became more and more apparent. Taking his case directly to the people, the president pounded away at the vulnerabilities of the GOP position. He emphasized his own commitment to a balanced budget with a tax cut while pleading for the preservation of the holy quartet of programs especially popular with the public—Medicare, Medicaid, education, and the environment. In contrast, the GOP's presentations were confused, technical, and off-message.

Clinton prevailed because he used the Fifth Estate tools of direct communication. He was able to speak over the heads of the press directly to the people—with one voice, compellingly, directly, and eloquently—to publicize his case and push the right buttons.

Congress comes across as discordant. The media used to be able to cover for Congress, lending it a coherence in print that it lacks up close. But on cable television there is nothing to clean up Congress's act. It looks chaotic, tempestuous, dilatory, and unfocused. As we watch the president each night, he looks directed, coherent, and purposeful by comparison.

While Congress, in its institutional bid for power, had replicated the technical tools of the administration through the Congressional Budget Office, it had failed to offset the political tools of the president—daily polling and paid advertising. Inexorably, the administration's emphasis on direct communication moved the balance of the battle in its favor.

For their part, congressional Republicans, smarting from their defeat over the budget, seized on Clinton's sexual indiscretions with Monica Lewinsky and his heavy-handed attempts to lie about them to press their quest for institutional dominance. In the unimpeachment the issues were sexual and legal, not financial and programmatic, but the stakes were the same as they had been in the budget fight: would the executive branch or the Congress prevail?

This presidency, a Fifth Estate institution, controlled and dominated the dialogue in a way that Congress could not hope to duplicate. The image of a president leading America, fighting for better schools, managing the economy, and standing up to Iraqi dictator Saddam Hussein resonated deeply with the American people. By contrast, the House of Representatives, torn apart by partisan debate and wrangling, came across as a lynch mob. The smooth coordination of the president's statements and his lawyers' tactics contrasted with the bitter denunciations of one another that dominated the congressional proceedings.

America saw members of its House of Representatives in action and was revolted by the image they projected on television. That these ferocious, rapacious men and women ran the country defied credibility. Every day on cable television, the House projected an image that was more typical of the Congress of a banana republic than of the United States.

When the nation's focus shifted to the Senate, the legislators themselves were muzzled by the rules of the proceedings. As the senators listened in silence, the House impeachment managers dueled with the president's lawyers. But the House proceedings had so taxed public patience that the senators felt under enormous political pressure to truncate the proceedings. As a result, the House prosecutors never really got to present their case. Denied the right to call witnesses, the House managers had to rely on videotaped depositions to make their case. In the end the president won a resounding victory. So total was the defeat of the House impeachment charges, and so extensive were the Republican Senate defections, that neither count of the impeachment could muster even a bare majority of the Republican-controlled Senate.

Democratic senators and the administration spokespeople aimed their comments perfectly, using the polling data the White House provided. The Congress, by contrast, did not poll and was flying blind. Anxious to avoid the lynch-mob atmosphere of the House proceedings, Senate Republicans' sound bites lacked any real punch. When the president delivered his magnificent State of the Union address and bombed Iraq right in the middle of the impeachment process, the contest became even more one-sided.

In the contest between the White House and Congress, it wasn't even a fair fight. The president had all the cards.

· · ·

The unimpeachment revealed a Congress in which a great deal took place that was of no relevance to us. In an Internet democracy, political figures will be exposed in the same way year round.

As the Fifth Estate evolves, Congress's power will diminish even more. The Fifth Estate's demand for direct communication, and its distaste for partisanship and special interests, will clip the wings of Congress further.

Epilogue

BUDDHIST PHILOSOPHER Thich Nhat Hanh writes that a flower is composed of "non-flower" elements. "When we look into the heart of a flower, we see clouds, sunshine, minerals, time, the earth and everything else in the cosmos in it. Without the clouds, there could be no rain, and there would be no flower. Without time, the flower could not bloom. In fact, the flower is made entirely of non-flower elements."

If the flower of which Thich Nhat Hanh writes is composed of non-flower elements, the unimpeachment of Bill Clinton consisted of much more than just the law and testimony. In the emerging era of the Fifth Estate, it demonstrated our national values and priorities, our attitudes toward the law, our views of sexuality, our opinions of the presidency, our sense of ethics, and our thinking about politicians and the media.

The impeachment debate gave us a detailed portrait of the core attitudes of the American people. Long after the controversies about our forty-second president have faded into history, the unimpeachment of 1999 will long be remembered as the moment when our national character was most evident and our deepest feelings most fully revealed.

What we discovered about ourselves was that we want to hold power in our own hands. And we can do so through the Internet.

.   .   .

In an agrarian economy one spoke of the grass roots of our politics. In the industrial age it was the factory floor that served as the resonant sounding board. Today it is the cyberroots. Voters will be galvanized by the Internet and empowered through their computers as never before.

The new world of the Fifth Estate and Internet politics will alter the very landscape of our politics. Money will matter less. Campaigns will have to become more user-friendly, interactive, and attractive. Voter turnout will rise as the opportunities for interaction increase. Politicians will have to listen more—a lot more—to the people.

How ironic that the most modern of tools, the Internet, should so catalyze our progress toward the oldest of visions: direct democracy. In some ways these changes will seem like a return to earlier ideas and strategies. Grassroots organizing will pick up where it left off. What small size and intimate geography permitted ancient Athens to accomplish, the Internet will let America and the world accomplish.

About the Author

Dick Morris grew up in New York City and graduated from Columbia College. He began his political career working in Democratic Party politics on Manhattan's Upper West Side. In the mid-1970s he began consulting for New York State Democrats such as Congresswoman Bella Abzug and Mayors Ed Koch and David Dinkins. His long association with President Clinton began in the late 1970s and continued for twenty years. Mr. Morris is often credited with the strategies that led to Mr. Clinton's move to the center of the political spectrum and his reelection in 1996. He has also worked as an advisor to Senate Majority Leader Trent Lott and other Republicans. *Time* magazine referred to him as "The most influential private citizen in America . . . a gleeful genius."

Dick Morris lives with his wife, the lawyer Eileen McGann, in Connecticut and New York City.

Additional Dick Morris Titles Available from Renaissance Books

Vote.com

ISBN: 1-58063-105-3 • $22.95

The New Prince

ISBN: 1-58063-079-0 • $22.95

Behind the Oval Office

ISBN: 1-58063-053-7 • $16.95

Also available from Audio Renaissance

Vote.com

Read by the author

ISBN: 1-55927-561-8 • $17.95

The New Prince

Read by the author

ISBN: 1-55927-542-1 • $17.95

Behind the Oval Office

Read by the author

ISBN: 1-55927-534-0 • $16.95

To order please call
1-800-452-5589